Does my Mom Have Dementia?

How to Recognize and Deal
with Dementia in Your Loved Ones

ERIK LANDE, PH.D. AND ROBERT DUFF, PH.D.

First edition

INTRODUCTION   1

WHAT IS DEMENTIA?   3

NORMAL AGING   13

The Aging Brain   14

Thinking Changes as We Age   19

IDENTIFYING DEMENTIA: WHAT TO LOOK FOR   24

Behavioral Signs   27

Thinking Changes   30

Language Changes (Aphasia)   35

TYPES OF DEMENTIA   43

Cortical Dementias   44

Subcortical Dementias   71

CONDITIONS THAT CAN LOOK LIKE DEMENTIA   87

Delirium   88

Nutritional Deficiencies   91

Normal Pressure Hydrocephalus   94

Adverse Medication Side Effects   95

Pseudodementia and Emotional Issues   97

WORKING WITH DOCTORS FOR A DIAGNOSIS — 100

The Initial Workup — 101

Dementia Doctors — 104

Diagnosis — 107

Relating to Doctors — 115

Ongoing Care — 118

CURRENT TREATMENTS AND BEHAVIORAL TOOLS — 120

Dementia Medications — 121

Active Learning Strategies — 123

General Memory Strategies — 125

Treatment of Mood Issues — 130

Behavioral Support — 132

DEMENTIA PREVENTION — 135

PROGNOSIS: WHAT TO EXPECT — 141

COPING WITH THE DIAGNOSIS — 146

LIVING WITH SOMEONE WHO HAS DEMENTIA — 155

TAKING CARE OF YOURSELF AS A CAREGIVER — 162

CONCLUSION — 171

1

Introduction

Hello! We're so glad you're here. Many of you reading this right now are going through a difficult time. Perhaps you are feeling worried, overwhelmed, concerned, or just confused about changes you're seeing in your parent or loved one. We completely understand. There is a great deal of unclear and downright scary information out there regarding the aging process and the complications that sometimes come along with getting older.

Our names are Erik Lande and Robert Duff. We're licensed neuropsychologists from Southern California, where we specialize in evaluating people from all walks of life to determine (among other things) whether they have dementia.

Did you know dementia and Alzheimer's disease are not the same thing? Did you know there are dozens of disorders that can cause memory impairment in older adults? Did you know that some of these disorders continue to worsen, while others stay relatively stable and some are even reversible? These are just a few of the topics we will help you understand in this book. Our intention is to take some of the fear and mystery out of the process of identifying dementia in your older loved ones. We will help you understand what types of changes are normal for the aging process as well as the warning signs of dementia and other memory issues. There is nothing worse than raising a concern about your loved one's behavior, only for them to get upset at you and write it off as "getting old." Allow us to clarify the situation plainly so you can avoid undue confrontation and move on with the important part: **doing** something about it.

In addition to clarifying the difference between normal aging and the dementia process, we'll explain the different types of dementia. Unfortunately, dementia can be a complicated beast with many unique presentations. Fortunately for you, there are easily identifiable clues that can help you understand exactly what's causing the type of difficulties you see. If you determine there may be cause for concern, we will help you navigate the waters of getting medical help. We appreciate that it's hard to know where to begin when it comes to getting help for a person in your life that may be suffering from dementia. Beyond that, terms like neurologist, neuropsychologist, and psychiatrist can create massive confusion among people who are not medical or mental health professionals. This book will offer plainly stated explanations of the different care providers and ideas on who you should be talking to about each issue. Lastly, we will discuss how you can best interact with someone who might be experiencing dementia and what you should be doing to take care of yourself.

If you feel you already have a good handle on dementia in general and would like to skip to a section that sounds more immediately useful for you, please do. However, we have found there is often more to learn about the concept of dementia, even for those who have already been through it with a loved one. So, once you are done going through the most relevant chapters, consider coming back to read the earlier chapters.

Without further preamble, let's dive in. The next section will focus on defining dementia and describing what issues would qualify someone for that diagnosis.

2

What is Dementia?

Let's start with the most obvious question: What in the world is dementia? In our experience, most people have a general understanding of dementia based off people they have seen in their lives or from movies and television. Often, they talk about someone they know who "lost it" in their old age or paint the stereotypical picture of someone with Alzheimer's disease forgetting the names of their own children. These descriptions *can* be representative of someone with dementia, but the truth is that dementia has many different forms and levels of severity. The term "dementia" itself is frequently misunderstood. Most people think it refers to one specific disorder when, in fact, it's simply a description of how someone is functioning. Dementia is not a disease or condition. Dementia can be *caused* by various diseases or conditions. Don't worry, we will make sure this is completely clear.

Plain and simple, dementia is the term that is used when someone has experienced a major loss of their thinking skills (including but not limited to memory) and this loss is now affecting their daily life in a significant way. Technically speaking, it means they are experiencing impairment that's worse than about 97 percent of their peers of the same age. Of course, there is some loss of functioning that happens with age, but in dementia this loss goes beyond what would be expected for a person's age level. This impairment can take a variety of forms. For instance, if a person has memory loss for recent events and can't remember to pay bills or attend important appointments, this might qualify them for a diagnosis of dementia. A more severe example might be someone who starts to lose weight because they don't remember that family members are leaving meals in the refrigerator for them. Another example would be a person that has begun to drastically slow in their processing speed, which is their ability to do basic tasks quickly. If this has impaired their ability to drive, since they aren't able to quickly make safe decisions while on the road, this could be another case where the diagnosis of dementia might fit the bill. Notice that in this last case, memory is not the skill that is causing them the most difficulty in daily life. Despite the public perception of dementia, memory is not always the greatest concern.

We'll get deeper into the different causes and types of dementia later. The most important thing to remember is that dementia is a description of functioning and it only tells you that the person has reached a certain level of impairment. It doesn't tell you anything about what exactly that impairment looks like or how it will progress. A good analogy would be to think of the term "learning disability." When someone says they have a learning disability, you have a general understanding of what they mean. They are describing issues with school-type skills and saying those issues interfere with their life. However, that does not explain what specific *type* of learning disability they are struggling with. Again, both dementia and learning disability are simply categories that describe the level or broad type of impairment.

Dementia is a category of functioning that means someone has impairment in their thinking skills (like memory) that is bad enough to significantly interfere with their functioning in daily life. There are many diseases or medical issues that can cause someone to have dementia. Alzheimer's disease is the most common disease that leads to dementia.

While the basic concept of dementia is fairly simple to understand, people have had difficulty wrapping their heads around it for ages, and the formal definitions have certainly changed with time. It's generally understood that the ancient Greeks were well ahead of their time in many ways. These geniuses had plumbing, showers, alarm clocks, democracy, and basic medicine, thousands of years ago. They also had the clarity to understand that there are different forms of thinking impairment that can occur. For instance, they made the distinction between delirium, which referred to a temporary state of confusion or impairment, and dementia, which referred to a condition that would persist over time. From there, though, things got muddled a bit.

Medical progress throughout history rarely follows a straight line. In the Dark Ages (the 5th to the 15th century), we decided that when people get old, they inevitably become "senile." This is a term that is not used so much anymore, but at the time it was thought that everyone will eventually go senile if they live long enough. It was a very stigmatized condition that was thought to be punishment for original sin. We won't bore you with a history lesson, but you can probably guess that people who were deemed senile were not treated very well during this period.

Luckily, we now know much more about the changes to the brain that come along with aging. Obviously, some degree of impairment happens as a normal part of the aging process, but certain people wind up much more impaired than others. In fact, the Alzheimer's Association has reported that one out of every three seniors will have some form of dementia at the time of their death. Looking specifically at dementia of the Alzheimer's type, the Association reports that more than five million Americans currently have Alzheimer's disease. This number is expected to grow in the coming years as the baby boomer generation begins to reach older adulthood. A 2013 study conducted at the Rush Institute for Healthy Aging in Chicago estimated that the number of people with Alzheimer's disease will climb to over 13 million by 2050.

In the field of psychology, we use a book called the Diagnostic and Statistical Manual of Mental Disorders (we usually just say DSM) to categorize and diagnose mental problems. The DSM represents an attempt to move away from stigmatization and toward a more scientific understanding of psychiatric conditions. A committee of hundreds of international mental health experts used a statistical approach to describe common mental disorders rather than just making intuitive guesses. Though terms like senility were no longer used, the earlier versions of the DSM still placed a heavy focus on dementias like the Alzheimer's type that are largely related to aging and memory concerns. This early focus on one particular category of dementia has likely contributed to the widespread misconception that Alzheimer's disease and the syndrome of dementia refer to the same thing. The current version of the Manual (DSM-V) is much broader and describes a variety of impairments that can happen at any age.

The DSM-V is still somewhat recent at the time of writing this book, but we did want to mention some of the newer terminology you may encounter. Unfortunately, the official terminology for the type of impairment we've been talking about has become a little more confusing to people who are not in the fields of psychology or medicine. Instead of using the term dementia, they now use the term "neurocognitive disorder." It sounds complicated, but if you break the term down, it just refers to problems in thinking that originate in your brain. Basically, the terms dementia and major neurocognitive disorder are interchangeable. The "major" part of that label refers to the fact that the difficulties are causing issues in daily living (as opposed to "mild" in which there is minimal functional impairment).

The other requirements for major neurocognitive disorder are a cognitive decline in at least one thinking domain, such as memory, complex attention, or language, and that these difficulties are not due to another mental disorder or medical condition. This means that a temporary state of impairment due to medication side effects would not qualify as dementia or major neurocognitive disorder. Likewise, if your elderly loved one just recently suffered the loss of their spouse and was understandably out of sorts for a while, but returned to normal functioning eventually, they would not have dementia either. We want to stress to you that currently, many health practitioners do not consistently use the new terminology. Most people will still use the term dementia to describe this type of impairment. Don't get tripped up. They mean the same thing.

DSM-V Criteria for Major Neurocognitive Disorder

A. Evidence of significant cognitive decline from a previous level of performance in one or more cognitive domains (complex attention, executive function, learning and memory, language, perceptual-motor, or social cognition) based on:

1. Concern of the individual, a knowledgeable informant, or the clinician that there has been a significant decline in cognitive function; and
2. A substantial impairment in cognitive performance, preferably documented by standardized neuropsychological testing or, in its absence, another quantified clinical assessment.

B. The cognitive deficits interfere with independence in everyday activities (i.e., at a minimum, requiring assistance with complex instrumental activities of daily living such as paying bills or managing medications).

C. The cognitive deficits do not occur exclusively in the context of a delirium.

D. The cognitive deficits are not better explained by another mental disorder (e.g., major depressive disorder, schizophrenia).

There is another related term that you may hear thrown around in doctors' offices called "mild cognitive impairment," or MCI. This refers to impairment that is greater than expected for someone's age level but not bad enough to meet criteria for dementia. This means that the person may have some degree of impairment in memory or other important thinking skills, but their level of impairment is not severe enough to cause a major functional impact in their daily life. For example, a person with MCI might have a hard time finding the word they are looking for, but they are typically able to find it when given enough time to think, whereas a person with dementia may never come up with the word. Another individual with MCI may forget a recent conversation or ask for clarification on the date for an upcoming event, whereas an individual with dementia may forget the event entirely and claim they were never told about it. MCI has become a very important term in the past 20-30 years because it is generally considered to be a transitional stage between normal thinking abilities and dementia. Therefore, there has been an increase in focused treatment during this stage with the hope of preventing dementia.

DSM-V Criteria for Mild Neurocognitive Disorder
A. Evidence of modest cognitive decline from a previous level of performance in one or more cognitive domains (complex attention, executive function, learning and memory, language, perceptual motor, or social cognition) based on:
   1. Concern of the individual, a knowledgeable informant, or the clinician that there has been a mild decline in cognitive function; and
   2. A modest impairment in cognitive performance, preferably documented by standardized neuropsychological testing or, in its absence, another quantified clinical assessment.
B. The cognitive deficits do not interfere with capacity for independence in everyday activities (i.e., complex instrumental activities of daily living such as paying bills or managing medications are preserved, but greater

effort, compensatory strategies, or accommodation may
be required).
C. The cognitive deficits do not occur exclusively in the
context of a delirium.
D. The cognitive deficits are not better explained by another
mental disorder (e.g., major depressive disorder,
schizophrenia).

Current estimates are that about 5–25 percent of older adults have MCI, and the incidence increases as they age. Their chances of transitioning into dementia also increase each year that they continue to struggle with MCI. MCI represents an important warning sign because it lets us know that something seems to be wrong and should at least be monitored if not treated outright. Currently the MCI population has become a major focus of drug research, as the goal is to stave off dementia before it fully develops. Regarding the terminology that we described above from the DSM V, mild cognitive impairment can also be called "mild neurocognitive disorder." Again, the "mild" part of that diagnosis acknowledges the impairment is not currently causing serious limitations in the person's daily living activities. Just remember dementia = *major* neurocognitive disorder and mild cognitive impairment (MCI) = *mild* neurocognitive disorder.

So far, we have referred to dementia in a very general sense. This is intentional. We are going to talk more about the different causes of dementia and what to expect with each type in a later chapter. For now, just know that there are many different causes of dementia, such as diseases of the brain, exposure to toxic substances, or even brain damage acquired through an accident. Dementia can look quite different depending on the exact cause, and we devote an entire chapter later to explaining those differences.

What's the big deal about dementia? Why are we so concerned about identifying it in the first place? Many people adopt the mindset that dementia is inevitable and there is little point in trying so hard to identify it. The fact is that dementia is not a fun process to deal with, but it does tend to go more smoothly when you identify it early and plan accordingly. Treatment for dementia is not cheap. The Alzheimer's Association estimates that medical care for individuals with dementia costs over $287,000 on average during the last five years of their life. Beyond that, families end up spending a great deal of their time caring for the individual with dementia. In fact, caregivers in the United States provide approximately 18 billion years of unpaid care each year. This is not surprising, since families will typically do whatever it takes to make sure their loved ones are not suffering and can live the best life possible, even if that means sacrificing their own time and money. However, being knowledgeable about symptoms, resources, and treatments available for dementia can help to ease this burden and prevent families from wasting time and money on ineffective strategies.

Hopefully at this point we've given you a baseline understanding of dementia in general. All this information is well and good, but what happens when your loved one begins to display some worrying behaviors and you aren't quite sure if you are just being oversensitive? It can absolutely be difficult to distinguish the normal difficulties that occur with aging from dementia or MCI if you don't know what to look for. Obviously, you don't want to upset the aging person in your life by jumping the gun and overreacting when there may not be cause for concern. However, many elderly people become quite skilled at compensating for their difficulties or making excuses for their behavior. Maybe you've already encountered the situation where your loved one blames their memory lapses on being retired or claims they couldn't find their keys because their spouse moved them. While we don't expect you to become diagnostic experts about dementia, we do want to arm you with enough knowledge to know when you should and shouldn't be concerned. In the next chapter we will talk all about normal aging and what benchmarks you should be using to judge your loved one's behavior and thinking skills

Case Studies:
These case studies are meant to illustrate a picture of what dementia and mild cognitive impairment actually look like in "real life." These (and all of the following) are not specific individuals we have worked with in our practice, but an amalgamation of different issues and individuals.

Case #1 (Mild Cognitive Impairment): Jenny is a 70-year-old woman who lives alone in her longtime home. She planned on retiring from her job as a program manager for a nonprofit organization at age 65. However, due to a lack of suitable replacement and Jenny's continuing need for an income, she still works full-time. As she has advanced in age, Jenny has begun to worry about her memory and overall cognitive state. She tends to become more overwhelmed by her numerous tasks at work and has recently made minor mistakes such as forgetting to put the stamp on an envelope and missing an online meeting due to a time zone difference. While Jenny tends to be quite hard on herself and admits to being stressed in general, those very close to her have started expressing concerns about her memory. Jenny continues to successfully live alone. She prepares many of her own meals, manages her medications without issue, and is quite conscientious about following through with commitments and appointments.

Case #2 (Dementia): Rick is a 67-year-old man who lives with his wife in a home in a retirement community. Rick and his wife sold their home and moved 200 miles away to downsize and purchase a home in their current retirement community two years ago. Even though they have been residents of their community since then, Rick continues to express confusion about directions and sometimes gets lost on the way to familiar locations such as the grocery store. He also frequently has difficulty recalling the date or

11

day of the week. When confronted with these issues, Rick will often blame retirement, stating that he "has no reason to keep track of these things." Rick's wife began expressing significant concern to his doctor following a troubling event in which Rick was found 12 miles from home, walking on the side of the highway. Upon being picked up by the police, Rick was quite dehydrated and exhibited serious confusion. After investigating the situation, it became clear that Rick started walking to a doctor's appointment and while he was walking, forgot where he was going. As a result, he continued walking in the same direction, which was toward his old place of residence.

3

Normal Aging

Before we get into specifics about the impairment that comes from different types of dementia, it's important to clarify the *normal* things that occur during aging. If you're eager to learn more about a specific type of dementia, feel free to jump forward a bit. However, we believe that having a good foundational knowledge about normal aging can help you better identify the warning signs of dementia **and** avoid "false positives" that could cause you to overreact to changes that are completely normal for the aging process. In general, the cognitive changes that come along with aging make a lot of sense because they essentially mirror the physical changes that happen in the body. Let's start this section off by talking about the normal physical changes that happen throughout the body as we age. Apologies in advance if this rings a bell for you personally… just remember these are *normal* changes and we all go through them.

You've probably noticed that, as humans, our bodies start to look pretty different as we get older. There is a great deal of variation, but in general it's common to see a little weight gain and some loss of muscle in older adults. The reason for this is not just that they might live a more sedentary lifestyle or become lazy once they retire. The human body's metabolism slows as we age because we require less energy. Metabolism is basically the process that our bodies use to convert the calories we take in through food into fuel for our bodies. After about 45 years, our bodies start to use fewer of those calories. This is partially due to loss of muscle mass (any meathead will tell you that muscle burns a lot of calories) and also because our internal organs become less needy and do not use up as much energy as before. The result is that an aging individual will tend to engage in less strenuous activity and require fewer calories to fuel their body. If this person continues to consume a similar diet to their 20- to 30-year-old self, they will inevitably gain weight. Interestingly, a similar effect happens in the brain. In our brains, we use a fuel called glucose (basically sugar). Just like our overall metabolism, the rate at which our brain can convert that glucose into usable energy also decreases. That means we have less energy and resources available for important thinking skills like memory and concentration. This is why it might take you a little longer to find your keys when leaving the house as you approach middle age.

The Aging Brain

Before we dive into how our brain changes, let's briefly discuss how it works. Our brain is an amazing organ powered by a vast network of interconnected cells called neurons. You've probably seen what neurons look like in cheesy animations on TV. Neurons are the cells that spread out like roots of a tree. We have about 100 billion neurons in the brain, and they work together to enable all our intentional and automatic behaviors. We don't need to dive super deep into neuroanatomy here, but you should at least understand that neurons work by shooting electrical and chemical impulses to one another. The space between two neurons is called the synapse and that's where chemicals are transferred back and forth. The chemicals within that synapse space are referred to as neurotransmitters because they *transmit* information between cells. Very important stuff. (Two neurotransmitters you may have heard of: dopamine and serotonin.)

If you don't have enough neurons in the brain, or those neurons are not functioning as well as they should, you can run into all sorts of different thinking difficulties. When it comes to aging, research shows that our decreased metabolism within the brain seems to cause something called atrophy. Atrophy can happen in any part of the body. It essentially refers to a decrease in the number of cells, causing a shrinkage. In the brain, atrophy presents as a loss of neurons as well as a loss of those synapse spaces between them. That means there are fewer neurons to draw upon and the connections between them also start to become altered, which leads to poorer communication between neurons. In a normally aging person this *does not* cause huge losses of functioning like you see in dementia. Our brain has many redundant backups built in that can compensate for these changes in a normally functioning person. Instead, these neurological changes lead to minor lapses here and there that are typically not cause for concern.

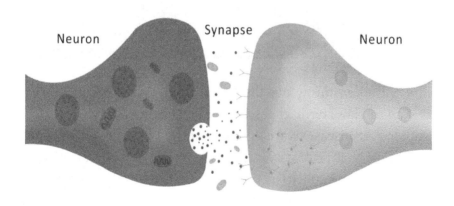

It's not only our metabolism that changes as we age. Decreased cardiovascular health is common in older adults. Loss of efficiency is the name of the game here as well. As we age, it becomes harder for our hearts to move blood around the body. Less energy and oxygen go to important muscles in the body, which leads to an overall sense of fatigue. Maybe you've noticed that skin changes with age as well. Specifically, we tend to bruise more easily, and our skin becomes less stretchy. The same thing happens in our brain. The blood vessels within our brain become less elastic and can develop atherosclerosis, which is a buildup of plaque within the blood vessels. This plaque blocks the flow of blood and contributes to that overall decrease in efficiency we were talking about.

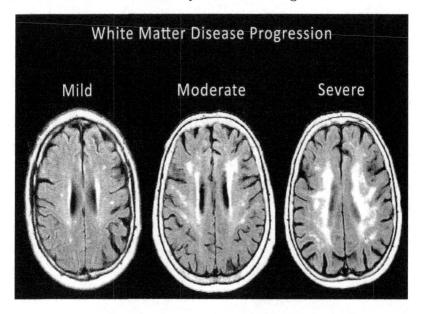

Doctors will often throw out the term "white matter disease." This is another one of those terms that sounds scary, but we all have some degree of white matter disease as we age. Also known as small vessel ischemic disease, white matter disease essentially means that the blood vessels within the brain are not circulating nutrients the way they should, which leads to damage of the brain tissue. The term "white matter" refers to the myelin sheath, which is a fatty substance surrounding the cells in our brain that helps neuron impulses move more quickly and efficiently. Putting this all together, white matter disease means that inefficiency within the brain's blood vessels leads to some damage of the tissue in the brain, especially in that myelin sheath (white matter). On an MRI scan it usually looks like white splotches. After age 60, it's normal to have some degree of white matter disease, which can make thinking somewhat slower and less efficient, but **too** much white matter disease can contribute to actual cognitive impairment. Someone with a history of high blood pressure or diabetes would be at higher risk for having a problematic level of white matter disease due to poorer overall cardiovascular health.

On a positive note, you can help your body resist these changes. You've likely heard that physical exercise is good for your brain. That's not just a scare tactic to get you to pay for an expensive gym membership. Research has clearly demonstrated that you can improve your metabolism and blood flow by engaging in frequent cardiovascular exercise, which we discuss further in Chapter 9: Dementia Prevention. Your brain benefits from this overall increase in efficiency as well, and it's becoming clear that regular physical activity can help slow the progression of white matter disease. Even if you've already undergone some decrease in cerebrovascular (blood vessels in the brain) health, exercise can prompt your body to grow new blood vessels and regain some functioning.

Brace yourself. If you're over 40 years old, sorry to say that your brain is already starting to shrink. After about age 40, humans begin to lose neurons in the brain, which literally causes it to shrink bit by bit. This is the atrophy we referred to earlier. We can still make new connections between neurons, learn new skills, and function within the world, but we all inevitably slow in our thinking abilities at some point.

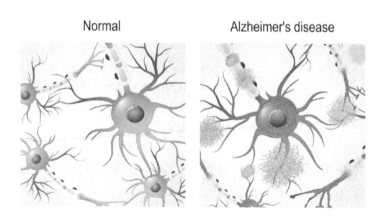

As if a shrinking brain wasn't bad enough, we also have some intruders in our brains that start to interfere with its functioning. Beta-amyloid plaques are nasty little clumps of fatty deposits and protein fragments that get stuck between neurons and reduce their ability to communicate with one another. These plaques can also cause inflammation within the brain that may damage those all-important neurons. There is also a protein in neurons called tau that normally helps with the cell's inner transportation system. During aging, this protein can build up or work in abnormal ways, which causes cells to collapse in on themselves and die. As neurons die and decay, they turn into neurofibrillary tangles, which as you can probably guess are not helpful for your thinking abilities. Typically, these neurofibrillary tangles first pop up in the portion of the brain that is responsible for learning and memory, which is probably why memory is such a common area of impairment for so many aging people. Again, a certain amount of these changes is normal for any aging person, but in some dementias, such as those caused by Alzheimer's disease, we see a much greater number of these beta-amyloid plaques and neurofibrillary tangles.

Abnormal Buildups in the Brain	
Beta-Amyloid Plaques	Clumps of fatty deposits and protein fragments that stick between neurons, making their communication less efficient.
Tau	A protein that helps the cell's transportation system. Too much build up causes cells to collapse on themselves.
Neurofibrillary Tangles	The wreckage of dead neurons.

We used a lot of big words just now, but you honestly don't need to remember all the terms. We just wanted to name some of the normal changes within the brain that lead to the typical shifts in an aging person's thinking. Essentially, you only need to remember that it's normal for the brain to become less efficient with age. This is due to some physical changes that damage neurons or block their functioning. Typically, this will not cause major problems.

Thinking Changes as We Age

So far, we have mostly described all the scary-sounding physical changes that are normal in the aging process, but we have not quite detailed the differences in thinking that accompany them. You will most likely recognize many of these thinking changes, as you see them in most of the normal aging people in your daily life. The most significant change with aging is in the speed of information processing. Processing speed refers to how quickly you can take in information, make sense of it, and use it to respond to some sort of demand. Speed of processing underlies most of our other thinking skills as well. Fast intake and processing of information helps to increase the efficiency of memory, multitasking, and even language abilities. On the flip side, when you lose some of your information processing speed, these skills become more difficult to draw upon quickly and efficiently. For some people, this looks like being less able to keep up with multiple people in a complex and fast-paced conversation, whereas they once would have thrived in this sort of situation. Slowed processing speed might also make you take longer to think about a decision, such as your order at a restaurant. This overall slowing is what leads many people to become less "sharp" than they were in their earlier years. Again, this is a normal change that we all go through.

At a basic level, intelligence refers to someone's capacity to learn and apply knowledge and skills. A good way to think of it is as mental horsepower— what sort of capacity you have "under the hood" for learning and reasoning. Research generally divides intelligence into two different categories: crystallized and fluid intelligence. Crystallized intelligence is the type of intelligence you acquire over a lifetime and it stays relatively stable with age. Just imagine the difference between crystals and fluids— crystals are solid and stay stuck to whatever geological structure they form upon, while fluids like water change shape to fit any surface or container.

Crystallized intelligence refers to what you might call wisdom. As we learn information about the world through our experiences, knowledge tends to grow and stick around throughout our lifetime. This is possibly one reason that the Supreme Court of the United States is comprised of mainly older people. They have a wealth of knowledge and crystallized intelligence that they have gained throughout a long life and career. At their age they probably have lost some processing speed as we have talked about, but they are able to take their time and not rush decisions, which allows them to utilize the full extent of their wisdom.

Unlike crystallized intelligence, fluid intelligence does not tend to remain stable as you age. Fluid intelligence refers to our ability to use logic to solve new problems. If you've ever upgraded to a new phone or rented a car while on a trip, you have used fluid intelligence. You were not already familiar with those exact objects, but you were able to apply your intelligence and adapt to the familiar, but slightly different scenario. Through trial and error and noticing the similarities to other devices you have used, you were able to learn how to use the phone or operate the car. Unfortunately, this ability declines a bit as we age. The most common example of decreased fluid intelligence that we hear is when someone buys a new device for their parent such as a smartphone, computer, or TV streaming device, and they have a massively hard time trying to teach their parent how to use it. Given enough time and repetition, most elderly people can adapt and learn how to use new devices and gadgets, but their ability to quickly figure it out on their own becomes much worse than it was during their 20s and 30s. An aging loved one may blame it on how complicated new technology is. In reality the changing demands of new devices simply serve as a way to highlight their reduced fluid intelligence. This is partially why some older people seem stubborn and set in their ways. It's difficult for their brains to adapt to new situations and easy to keep the same routines and habits. Keeping good habits and routines is a great strategy at any age to reduce decision fatigue and improve your own efficiency, but it's the lack of flexibility in doing new things that creeps in as we get older.

Cognitive Domains Related to Aging	
Processing Speed	The speed with which you can take in information and efficiently process it. Plays a role in memory, communication, and higher-level thinking skills.
Crystallized Intelligence	Information and knowledge that you have accumulated over your lifetime. The skill that is required for trivia games.
Fluid Intelligence	Your ability to use logic and creatively solve new problems. Allows you to identify patterns and adapt.

There is a hypothesis put forth by people like Robert L. West (1996) that explains why this decrease in fluid intelligence happens in older adults while their crystallized intelligence remains mostly intact. It's called the Frontal Lobe Hypothesis and it essentially claims that the frontal area of the brain tends to age more quickly than the other parts of the brain. Evolutionarily, the frontal lobe is the part that tends to get bigger and bigger as animals become more complex. As humans, we have massive frontal lobes. This is for good reason. The frontal lobe of the brain is really what defines us as humans because it governs our ability to imagine hypothetical scenarios, to ignore distractions and focus on the most important aspects of our environment, to multitask, and to plan before acting. We call this group of skills "executive functioning." Just remember that the frontal lobe is the executive of your brain.

All those fun brain changes that we talked about in this chapter tend to occur faster in the frontal lobes than the other areas. This is easily evidenced by the fact that the volume of the brain decreases more in the prefrontal cortex (right behind your forehead) than any other region during the aging process. This means that of all the skills to be affected in a normally aging person, complex attention, multitasking, and planning are going to be the first to decline. It's no wonder your run-of-the-mill 80-year-old has such a hard time working a standard TV remote. To you it looks simple, but to someone with decreased executive functioning, it looks like a 40-button monster. Their frontal lobe is not letting them quickly filter out the unimportant buttons and visualize what worked for them with their previous remote control.

Here is a graphic to help you visualize this whole aging brain process:

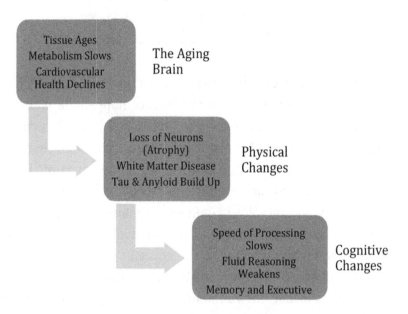

It can be scary to learn about all the nasty stuff that happens to your brain as you age. We have emphasized this plenty of times in this chapter, but it bears repeating one last time that these physical and cognitive changes are part of the **normal** aging process that everyone goes through to some extent. In an average person, these changes will not lead to a problematic loss of functioning. A normally aging person will still get by just fine without many significant limitations.

Case Study – Normal Aging

Erika is a 70-year-old woman who has worked as a university professor for the last 30 years. She is well-loved by her students and respected by her colleagues for her no-nonsense approach to teaching introductory psychology and sociology courses.

Erika has always been someone with a razor-sharp wit and high level of professional performance. This has made it all too apparent to her that she has started having some "senior moments," which she has been able to laugh about. Erika finds she sometimes walks into a room of her house, only to immediate forget what she was doing. Typically, the task at hand comes back to her once she starts to retrace her steps. She also has a habit of losing her keys and sunglasses, which sometimes causes her to rush out the door to make it to class on time. Once upon a time, Erika had no problem memorizing the names of the students in all her courses. These days, she relies on the class roster a little more to jog her memory.

Erika is not very concerned about her memory. She feels that compared to her peers around the same age, she is still similar or better. She sometimes remarks that she is finally starting to feel her age and may be looking to retire in the next few years.

Though the normal aging process is familiar to most people, it can be quite difficult to pick up on signs that there is something more going on. In the next chapter we talk all about the red flags and subtle signs that indicate there may be something worse than just normal aging going on.

4

Identifying Dementia:
What to Look For

Before we dive into the different signs and symptoms of dementia, we should talk a bit about why it matters in the first place. In our line of work, it's common for us to encounter friends and family of elderly people who don't see much value in identifying dementia or other cognitive issues. They often express something to the effect of, "What's the point of doing all this testing? There is no cure for Alzheimer's, right? What difference does it make to know for sure?" We certainly can't fault them for feeling this way. As we will talk about in a later chapter, the process of testing for dementia is not exactly fun, and family members are often hesitant to agitate their loved one unless there is a very good reason for it. However, we feel that there are indeed some good reasons for identifying dementia as early as possible. For one, it may not be dementia! Wouldn't it be great to discover that the thinking changes occurring in your loved one are not the result of irreversible dementia, but some other kind of cognitive impairment that can be solved with the correct treatment? A variety of disorders create difficulties in thinking that can look very similar to dementia, but when accurately diagnosed and treated they can be completely reversed, and the person can go back to their normal level of functioning. Even if the person does happen to be suffering from dementia of some type, as we mentioned at the beginning of this book, there are

24

many different types of dementia. While most forms of dementia are not reversible, in some cases, it's possible to keep someone at a higher level of functioning for longer if they are treated with the appropriate medication or intervention. We'll go through some of the specific types of dementia later in this book and you will see that each type has a different sort of progression and a unique pattern of difficulties. There is no "one size fits all" approach to dementia. It can be very helpful to identify which type of dementia you are looking at so you can provide the right sort of care and support.

So now that we have convinced you (hopefully) that it's important to catch and identify dementia, let's talk a bit about the warning signs you should keep in mind. These behavioral "red flags" are potentially cause for concern. Please keep in mind that you cannot diagnose someone based on these symptoms; rather, they are a starting point that tells you to dig deeper.

> "I don't need to know the date, I'm retired!"
> - Something we hear on a weekly basis, but a person really should know at least the month and the year

Are They Oriented?

When we, as neuropsychologists, assess an elderly person, the first thing we look at is whether they are "alert and oriented." The term "alert" is fairly self-explanatory: aware, engaged, and relatively clear of mind. Most people are not quite alert first thing in the morning when they've not yet had their coffee, but someone with dementia may have difficulty staying alert well into the day. Hallmark features are a blank facial expression, disheveled appearance, and overall confusion. You might notice that your loved one does not appear to be very engaged with conversations. Someone will typically nod their head, make sounds like "mhm" in agreement, or even ask questions to indicate they're actively participating in the conversation. Someone who is struggling with their ability to stay alert might seem more like they are "out of it" and stare blankly into space, or even "through" you rather than keeping normal, appropriate eye contact. This is less important if someone has always been passive in their conversational style. However, if they have typically been engaged and aware, it may be cause for concern if they adopt this less alert style later in life.

Regarding that passivity, the person may also become more dependent on others for answers. Rather than speak up themselves when asked a question, they may get in the habit of looking to their family, spouse, or caregivers to give the answer. A common scenario is that you ask the person, "So did you do anything exciting over the weekend?" and they respond, "Oh sure, we uh..." and they trail off and look to their spouse to fill in the details. On its own, this behavior is fairly benign, and you wouldn't think twice about it. But if you notice it happening regularly, it might be a sign that your loved one is trying to mask issues with their memory. It's important to remember they are likely not trying to be deceitful in covering up their memory problems, it's just embarrassing to have to say "I don't remember," and it's easy to fall into a natural pattern of relying on your spouse or family member to fill in the missing information.

Orientation is a medical term we use to refer to someone's knowledge of themselves and their external reality. Basically, we check to see if someone is "oriented to" four criteria: person, place, time, and situation. Being oriented to person means they are aware of their own biographical information, such as name, date of birth, address, and phone number. Orientation to place means they know where they are. Time orientation means someone knows the date, day of the week, and approximate time of day. Finally, orientation to situation means that someone understands what's happening in the immediate situation and why they are in a given place (say, at the doctor's office for a yearly checkup). Of the four categories, it is typically more obvious when a loved one is experiencing difficulty with orientation to person, because that means they are forgetting their own personal information. However, one of the most commonly overlooked issues is when a loved one begins to lose their orientation toward time. Without peeking at your computer, phone, or watch, can you say to yourself the month, date, year, and about what time of day it is? The vast majority of people can. If not, you are probably only off by one or two days on the date or perhaps have the wrong day of the week due to a holiday weekend or similar circumstance. Now, many people who are elderly and no longer working will have some excuse such as, "Oh I'm retired, and every day is the same now. I have no need to know the date!" While it's true they don't need to be as aware of the date as someone who is still in school or the workforce, a normally aging person will still have a pretty good sense of it. You can give them a little leeway on the exact date, but if they are hardly ever able to identify the month, or they don't know what year it is, it could be a sign they are experiencing cognitive difficulties.

Behavioral Signs

There are a variety of behavioral signs to look for in your loved one that may be indicative of a developing dementia process. As with all the other signs and red flags, these are mainly important if they are changes from their previous functioning. If they have always exhibited the behaviors that we'll discuss here, don't worry about it. It's when they develop new quirks, habits, and tendencies later in life that we need to be concerned. Many early behavioral signs of dementia have a repetitive nature to them. For instance, people with dementia will sometimes engage in the same motion over and over, such as folding or ripping paper. They might also start to scratch or pick at their skin. These behaviors seem to be compulsive in nature and the person might not even realize that they are doing it unless someone draws their attention to it. In some cases, repetitive behaviors

27

like scratching or picking can even cause scabs or bleeding. The picking type of behavior is very common, and it isn't always simply that the person picks at their skin. Rather, it might seem that they are constantly picking at lint, stray hairs, or other trivial nuisances on their clothing. In our practice, we often see repetitive behaviors during the interview with the patient. If the person has a purse or a bag, it is very common to see them constantly fiddle with it, opening and closing the zippers or clasps when asked a question. Likewise, they might pick at their nails or wring their hands when under pressure. These sorts of behaviors are often written off as nervous tics. While it's true that some people compulsively pick when they are experiencing stress or anxiety, you should take note if this is an unusual behavior for your loved one that they seemed to have developed more recently.

Have they always acted this way?
-   New quirks, habits, or perseverative behaviors can be a sign that something is not right

---

It can sometimes seem like a person with dementia is stuck on a loop that keeps playing out over and over. If the person is getting ready for an upcoming trip or even a short outing, they might get stuck in the loop of packing and unpacking their belongings many times over. These relatively minor behavioral signs can be hard to catch because they're often done in private. Let's say you are picking your loved one up for a doctor's appointment or family dinner. They may tell you to wait just a moment while they get their things together from their bedroom and next thing you know, 15 minutes have passed while they are packing and unpacking their belongings in confusion. When you realize that so much time has passed, you yell to them and ask if everything is okay, which prompts them to snap out of their loop and carry on. Repetitive behaviors are not always physical. Someone with dementia can also fall into verbal repetition. For example, you might ask them if they would like anything from the store and they say "no" and continue to mutter "no... no... no... no... no..." under their breath. Similarly, you might notice a person humming constantly. Of course, someone with memory concerns may repeat questions several times due to pure forgetting, but sometimes people who are not quite at that level of forgetfulness in their dementia will still ask questions over and over in a more compulsive fashion that fits with these other behaviors we've been talking about.

Other behavioral signs of dementia are related to mood and personality. Perhaps you've confronted your loved one about a lapse in their memory or some other concerning behavior, only to be met with anger or agitation. For a person who is beginning to decline in their cognitive abilities, it's hard for them to notice and admit when they are starting to show signs of decline. It's both embarrassing and confusing to have difficulties with your thinking skills. Which makes a lot of sense: Our brains are really our greatest allies as we move throughout the world and accomplish our goals. You grow accustomed to relying on your brain to function the way it's supposed to, so when you have little lapses in your thinking abilities, it can be quite shocking. Rather than recognize that there's a serious issue going on, the brain will sometimes rationalize and explain away the problem. This can lead to excuses, anger, denial, and frustration as your brain scrambles to find an alternative explanation for the issues that are occurring. A common example is for a person to blame their spouse for taking something when it was the person themselves who moved or hid the object in the first place. In some cases, your loved one may become overly defensive about small issues that you point out, whereas a normally functioning person would laugh and let the criticism slide. They might also point this frustration inward and become upset at themselves for what appear to be very minor mistakes.

One of the most common early behavioral quirks that people with dementia develop is a tendency toward isolation and withdrawing from normal social situations. This can be very confusing for family members, especially if the person is generally happy and has not typically had a tendency toward depression or extreme introversion. An individual who is beginning to develop dementia will begin to avoid social gatherings and other common outings due to cognitive difficulties. Let's imagine that this person is starting to develop difficulties keeping up with conversations and finding the correct word to say when speaking with others. They might be able to get by and cope well with one or two instances of difficulty in a conversation with a close family member. However, when they are in a more complex social situation, they'll be presented with many more opportunities for this difficulty to rear its head, which means they'll have to be more on guard and aware of their behavior. This can be exhausting and agitating, and to them it may begin to feel like it's just not worth the trouble. There is also the embarrassment factor to consider. We often work with individuals who have always been high performers in their field and now find themselves misspeaking about topics they should be familiar with while out with their peers. This causes them to avoid spending time with these peers for fear of making a fool of themselves. In some cases, the person may not be aware of the exact reason they don't want to go out and engage with others socially, but blame it on being tired or say they "just don't feel like it." This can evolve into a vicious cycle where the person appears to be depressed because they don't want to bother with the exhausting experience of being around others, then feel legitimately depressed due to their isolation.

Thinking Changes

The behaviors we've mentioned are fairly subtle and sometimes related to the thinking difficulties caused by dementia in a roundabout way. So, what about the actual cognitive problems that occur in dementia? What should you be looking out for to catch early signs of memory loss or other declines in thinking skills? The most important thing to keep in the back of your mind is that there are many different disorders that can cause dementia, and for each given type, the pattern of issues looks somewhat different. It is also essential to get a professional evaluation to fully understand what changes might be occurring in a loved one. That being said, let's talk about a few common difficulties you can spot in everyday situations.

Early signs of thinking difficulty are often annoying for spouses or other family members before they become outright problematic for the individual in their life outside of the home. Typically, a person who is developing dementia will not start with more severe memory problems such as forgetting to pay their bills or being unable to recall the name of their grandchild. Instead, they'll drive their family crazy by asking the same questions over and over. It's a mistake to think that the person is intentionally trying to be a nuisance, but that doesn't stop the situation from being frustrating. It is incredibly common for family and caregivers to become annoyed at repeating themselves constantly. The repetitive questioning can be for a variety of reasons. For one, reduced short-term memory can cause the person to not remember the information that they learned when they first asked the question. If the person has an issue with attention, the new information may not sink in in the first place, which would of course mean that they can't remember it later. If the person is having difficulty understanding spoken language, they may nod in agreement, but not truly process the meaning of what was said, which can lead them to ask for clarification later.

Are there repetitive stories or questions?
- Repetitive questions about upcoming or recent events can suggest that a person's brain is not processing information effectively

---

All these subtle difficulties can cause uncertainty in the individual, which might cause them to repetitively ask questions even if they have the correct information in the first place. Common questions to look out for include "When are we leaving?", "Who is coming over again?", "Did you buy our plane tickets?", "Where are you going?", and "When will you be coming back?" Having a lapse and asking for clarification every once in a while is perfectly normal. For instance, I (Dr. Duff) have always driven my wife crazy because I can never seem to remember when minor holidays like St. Patrick's Day or Valentine's Day are. Therefore, questions of that variety would not be considered a change for me. In contrast, if your loved one has always been the keeper of the calendar and is razor sharp when it comes to remembering people's birthdays, you may be right to be concerned that they keep asking you for the date of their child or sibling's birthday. That would be an unusual behavior for them that probably hints at a loss of previous functioning.

As mentioned, anxiety and uncertainty can interplay with these minor cognitive changes. The result of this combination is often a repetitive "checking" behavior. Rather than having faith in their own ability to retain information, they will begin to doubt the information in their own brain, which generates a sense of tension and unease. To reduce this tension, people who are developing dementia often fall into a loop of clarifying and checking information. This is very commonly seen when there is some upcoming event or activity that the person is concerned about missing. For example, if the person has a dinner to go to later in the evening, they might ask whether it is time to leave for the dinner many times throughout the day. To this, a spouse might continue clarifying, "No, dear. The dinner is at 6, so we will leave in a couple of hours." You can see how this might be frustrating for both parties. Rather than interpreting the behavior as the person being intentionally difficult or lazy, it's important to instead keep track of the behavior as a potential sign of cognitive decline. Keeping a physical notebook or using the notes application on your phone can be a helpful way to log how often and under what circumstances this type of behavior occurs.

Aside from upcoming events, a person who is developing dementia might forget recent conversations. In more mild cases, their memory for the particulars of the conversation may become fuzzy, or they might mix up the details with those from a different chat. In more advanced cases, they can completely forget a conversation. Among spouses, this can often lead to resentment because one party feels like they are not being heard or that the other person doesn't care about what they have to say. At other times, the person who is doing the forgetting might become agitated or angry because they feel quite certain they weren't told the information in the first place and don't appreciate being accused of forgetting. Denial and defensiveness are common in the early stages of cognitive impairment.

These small signs of memory loss and thinking changes stand in contrast to the typical changes mentioned in the previous chapter about normal aging. If your loved one has a tendency to walk into a room and forget why they went there, that is probably just a product of the normal aging process. Same goes for forgetting exactly where they parked in a large parking lot. This is something that naturally becomes more difficult with age and typically on its own is not cause for concern. Now, if the person in question walks into a room in their own home and has difficulty figuring out which room they are in, that's a different story. Similarly, if the person walks out of the store and can't remember whether they drove or walked there, that may be an indication that there are more than just simple aging changes occurring in their brain.

All the examples that we have given so far are related to recent memory. That's because, in general, a person who is developing dementia will frequently hold onto distant memories pretty well. You are unlikely to see someone in the very early stages of dementia forgetting where they went to high school or where they vacationed with their family as a young adult. These deeply rooted autobiographical memories are typically well preserved early in the development of cognitive impairment. It's certainly possible for someone with dementia to have difficulty recalling their main career or the name of their hometown, but these tend to occur in later stages. Therefore, these are typically not the types of issues that you need to be keeping an eye out for early on.

If you notice that your loved one seems to have a significant loss of distant memories and autobiographical information, it could be that they are either demonstrating momentary confusion or that their decline has occurred under the radar. This can sometimes happen when an elderly individual lives alone or with a similarly functioning spouse and their family only sees them on rare occasions such as holidays.

Normal Brain Aging	Problematic Brain Aging
Momentarily forgetting a word during conversation.	Forgetting a word and not being able to work around it, causing the conversation to halt.
Occasionally having a late fee from a bill that wasn't paid on time.	Having services shut off due to delinquent payments.
Forgetting the name of a distant relative.	Forgetting the name of an immediate family member.
Repeating a question or story once in a while.	Persistently repeating questions or stories several times per day.
Momentarily forgetting where the car is parked upon exiting a store.	Requiring assistance to find the car or leaving on foot without the car.

In these cases, it is possible to miss the early warning signs of dementia and instead see large leaps in memory decline. A good analogy is to think of a growing child. A parent will not usually notice growth in their child the same way that relatives who only see the child periodically do.

A similar phenomenon can happen with declining elders. We frequently hear stories in our clinical practice about family members who visit from out of town and are blindsided by how impaired their aging relative is.

> "Could you go to the garage and grab me the... uh.... the... you know the thing that you twist around?"
> - Any of us could have a word finding lapse, but if such difficulties seem above and beyond those of peers, it may be a sign something is wrong

Language Changes (Aphasia)

Memory is probably the most obvious area of decline in dementia and one of the easiest to notice in your loved one. Many people don't realize that language changes can be warning signs of cognitive difficulties. The term "aphasia" is used to describe impaired language skills. There are many different disorders that can cause aphasia, including dementia conditions. This is somewhat simplified, but there are essentially two varieties of aphasia: expressive and receptive. In basic terms, this means difficulty understanding language that is spoken to you (receptive) or difficulty accurately conveying thoughts verbally (expressive). Aphasia does not only apply to spoken language. In fact, you can have expressive or receptive aphasia that affects written language as well. Receptive aphasia can be somewhat difficult to distinguish from memory problems because the individual with aphasia may listen to someone speak and act as if they understand what is being said, when they are actually having marked difficulty processing the information. Therefore, when they are required to recall the information later, they may not be able to do so correctly. Logically, this would lead others in their life to assume that they forgot the information, but in this case the person didn't fully understand what was said in the first place. This can be tested by using "comprehension checks" and asking the person to paraphrase what they just heard. Please note that it is important to avoid asking yes or no questions such as "Did that make sense?" because the person will likely just say yes or nod in order to avoid an awkward situation. Rather, ask them to explain what was just said back to you in their own words so that you can be sure they understood. If they are consistently unable to give you the correct information, that may be an indication of early language impairment, which can be a warning sign for developing cognitive impairment.

Here's a scenario that should be familiar to most people: "Hey when you get home, could you go to the garage and grab me the... uh.... the... you know the thing that you twist around?" "You mean the wrench?" "That's the word!" This is an example of failed word-finding. Everybody has the occasional word-finding difficulty, especially as we age. However, an increase in word-finding problems above and beyond that seen in the individual's peers may be representative of that expressive aphasia we mentioned.

Word-finding deficits can sometimes be hard to spot because spouses, family members, or caretakers can fall into a pattern of covering for the person. Each time the person with cognitive difficulties forgets a word, their caretaker instantly swoops in and provides the correct response as to avoid unnecessary confusion. This pattern can sometimes involve the person physically looking to their spouse or caregiver for the answer. If you are the caregiver, family member, or spouse in this scenario, we encourage you to be aware of how often you come to the rescue with the correct word. Try refraining from providing the correct word to your loved one and note exactly how often the word-finding difficulty is happening. This can give you a better idea about whether it's normal behavior for their age or if it seems to be a legitimate concern. A normally aging person will typically remember the word when they are given some time to think or it might come back to them later in the day. For someone who has significant cognitive impairment, they may not be able to find the word, even when given time to think of it.

Loss of Insight

The most difficult part of identifying and confronting early cognitive decline in a loved one who may be developing dementia is their loss of insight into their own functioning. By this we mean they are not able to notice the same changes you are. Often in our clinical practice, we are most worried by those who come in and tell us they are completely fine. Logically, if you are concerned about your memory loss, that means you're at least cognitively sound enough to recognize there is an issue. In other words, you can remember that you sometimes forget things. However, when someone comes in and says "I don't know why I'm here. I do not have Alzheimer's. I am not going cuckoo!" we know to dig a little deeper.

> ### "Leave me alone, you're all crazy"
>
> - Dementia can limit a person's ability to understand what is happening to them. It is frustrating and confusing to everyone involved. Confronting it head-on often does not work.

Loss of insight can be incredibly frustrating and confusing for family members because it looks a lot like denial. When someone is in denial, they are aware of their difficulties at some level, but adamantly refuse to admit them. That is not what tends to happen with dementia. Instead, this is a scenario where the person literally cannot see the problem or does not have the capacity to understand what is happening to them. It's almost as though the brain has a blind spot. The reason they can't understand the issues they are experiencing is due to those very same issues clouding their awareness.

Understanding the difference between denial and a lack of insight can enable family and caregivers to be more forgiving and gracious with the person. It can be very tempting to constantly argue with the impaired individual and give them examples to prove them wrong. For instance, we frequently see family members saying something like "Mom... tell the truth. You forgot to take your medicine the entire week I was on vacation, remember?" Falling into a pattern of correcting your loved one and trying to convince them to recognize they are impaired can create an emotionally charged situation that is not helpful to anyone involved. Trying to drive the point home is most often a losing battle. Imagine trying to convince someone who is blind that they can actually see. Instead, consider working *within* their beliefs.

"Someone has been stealing my tissues"

- Some people with dementia lose touch with reality, experiencing delusions or hallucinations. Don't panic. Empathize with the distress they feel and gently direct them to focus on something else.

Rather than trying to convince them that they are wrong, just roll with their statements and try to remind them of the information or continue with the conversation as normal. Ask yourself what will be gained by arguing with them about the truth of the situation. In more extreme examples, such as a man constantly forgetting that his wife of 40 years died, it may do more harm than good to frequently remind him that he is alone. Every time he's informed of her death, he feels the pain again for the first time. Just remember that there is no perfect way to handle a loved one who has no insight into their condition. It can be taxing and frankly sad to pretend like everything's okay when it's not. Even though you don't want to get in the habit of arguing with the person, sometimes you need to make sure they are following through with their medications and attending important appointments, even if they don't believe they have a problem that requires medication or medical follow up. Use your familiarity with your loved one's personality to find the best way to gently guide them to the truth while avoiding conflict where possible.

Psychosis

Before we wrap up this chapter on dementia warning signs, we want to address one of the more worrisome symptoms you may encounter. People with dementia sometimes develop psychosis, which refers to experiencing the world differently than other people. Psychosis can come in two forms: hallucinations and delusions. Hallucinations are sensory experiences that most other people don't have: hearing or seeing things that are not there. You can also have hallucinations from other senses such as smell or taste, but those can be harder to spot.

Examples of hallucinations might be seeing children in the house when there are none or hearing music when it is silent. On the other hand, delusions are unusual thoughts that most other people do not have and that contradict reality. For example, the belief that you are a messiah or that people are out to get you would be instances of delusional thoughts.

The most common disorder that causes psychosis is schizophrenia, so it's totally understandable if it sounds a little scary. In dementia, though, delusions are often not all that bizarre. One of the most common is the belief that people are stealing your personal items. This can occur when the individual misplaces their clothes, jewelry, or food, then blames others for stealing them. We have seen patients who have literally chained their kitchen cabinets closed, as they believe someone is stealing food, when most likely they have eaten the food themselves and forgotten about it. This is another way the brain tries to rationalize the situation rather than acknowledge cognitive difficulties. In clinical practice we have also come across spouses who spontaneously begin to believe their partner has cheated on them when there is no evidence to support the idea. That isn't to say someone with dementia can't develop more bizarre and disturbing delusions, but those are typically easier for family members to catch. These smaller and more benign delusions are more likely to fly under the radar or be misinterpreted as emotional or relationship difficulties.

Psychosis Symptoms		
Hallucinations	Having sensory experiences of things that are not there (hearing, seeing, smelling, etc).	Examples: Hearing people talking in the walls when it's actually quiet or seeing figures standing in the room.
Delusions	A belief or reality that does not line up with other people's reality.	Examples: The belief that people are trying to poison you or feeling that your loved one has been replaced by a doppelgänger.

If your loved one seems to be experiencing psychosis in the form of delusions or hallucinations, don't panic. Rather than assume they have developed something like schizophrenia, check in with their doctor and report the symptom along with any of the other warning signs we've talked about in this chapter.

As with confronting someone with dementia about their lack of insight, trying to prove their delusional thoughts wrong might also be a losing battle. While you may not agree or experience reality the way they do, you can probably empathize with the worry or pain that it is causing and support them. Rather than start an argument, express concern about their discomfort and reassure them that everything will be okay soon. For example, if your loved one has the delusion that someone is trying to poison them, you don't need to argue about the reality of that. Instead, you can tell them you understand how scary that must be and offer to get them a fresh drink so they are sure it's not poisoned.

41

In Summary

The purpose of this chapter was to give you a broad overview of some symptoms and red flags that indicate the possible presence of dementia in your loved one. Remember that we're looking for areas of change from their previous functioning or personality. If they have always had an issue, that would not be evidence of decline in their abilities. Also, note that none of the symptoms presented here are sufficient to diagnose dementia. Instead, consider them to be a jumping-off point. If you notice a few of these red flags in your loved one, keep track of them in your physical or digital log and bring that information to the doctor to help point them in the right direction.

Now that we have covered the overall warning signs and red flags for dementia, let's go a little deeper. In the next chapter, we are going to look at some of the specific types of dementia and their unique patterns of behaviors and cognitive difficulties.

5

Types of Dementia

As we mentioned in the introduction, many people use Alzheimer's disease and dementia interchangeably. This makes sense, since Alzheimer's disease is currently the most common cause of dementia. It is a bit difficult to obtain an exact figure, but it appears that somewhere between 60 and 80 percent of all dementia cases are attributed to the effects of Alzheimer's disease. Since you're still reading this far into the book it's clear you want to know the differences between dementias. It's extremely useful to understand these differences because treatment often depends on the specific form of dementia in question. In some cases, the impairment may be reversible, meaning you can solve the issue with the right kind of treatment. So, let's look at some of the ways in which we can categorize dementia and explore some examples of specific disorders.

When identifying and treating dementia it's crucial to understand where in the brain the impairment is taking place. We would like to stay true to our promise of not putting you through an entire neurobiology lesson, but as with the chapter on normal aging, a little background information on the brain is necessary here. When you imagine the brain, you probably picture the typical illustration of a squishy pale-pink organ with lots of folds and ripples. That outer portion of the brain is called the cortex. The word cortex is Latin for "bark" or "shell" since that is the outer covering of the brain and all the folds sort of look like the bark on a tree. This bark basically includes all parts of the brain that are responsible for our larger, overarching skills like language, memory, and reasoning. The types of dementia that affect this portion of the brain are referred to as cortical dementias. Makes sense, right?

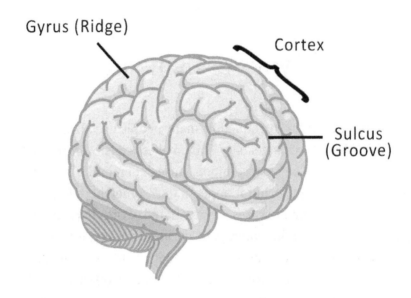

Gyrus (Ridge)

Cortex

Sulcus (Groove)

Cortical Dementias

Some main types of cortical dementias you may be familiar with are those resulting from Alzheimer's disease, frontotemporal degeneration, Lewy body disease, and mad cow disease. Remember, these are diseases that mainly affect that outer cortex of the brain and cause impairment in functioning that can be intense enough to be classified as dementia. Since these forms of dementia primarily affect the cortex, they involve impairment in those bigger overall skills such as memory or language. Because they affect the more obvious skills, cortical dementias can be easier to identify when interacting with the impaired person in everyday life. Next, we will dive a little deeper and explore some specific cortical dementias. Since Alzheimer's disease is the most well-known cause of dementia, let's start there.

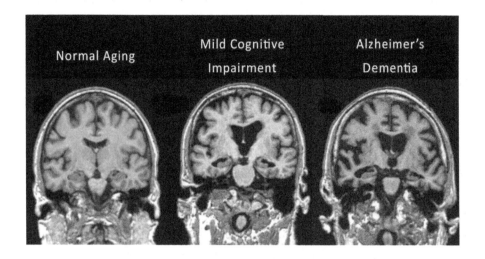

Alzheimer's Disease

Alzheimer's disease causes changes in the brain. Dementia of the Alzheimer's type describes when Alzheimer's disease causes cognitive impairment that is significant enough to be classified as dementia. Someone in the very early stages of Alzheimer's disease will not yet have dementia from it. You may have heard some folks refer to it as "old timer's," which makes logical sense since it is an age-related disorder, but that's just a misnomer. The disorder is named after a psychiatrist from the 1900s by the name of Alois Alzheimer who first described the symptoms of the disorder.

You are probably familiar with some of the main symptoms of Alzheimer's disease, but what actually happens to the brain? Basically, Alzheimer's causes a breakdown of the neurons. For this reason, we would refer to it as a neurodegenerative disease. "Neuro" refers to the brain and "degenerative" refers to deterioration over time. This neurodegeneration causes the brain to atrophy, which can be seen plainly in MRI imaging. In addition to the physical deterioration, when you look at the brain of an

Alzheimer's patient during an autopsy, you see lots of those amyloid plaques and neurofibrillary tangles that we talked about in the chapter on normal aging. Essentially, it's a more severe version of the normal aging process that affects specific regions in the brain.

There are a few key areas of the brain that Alzheimer's disease seems to target. The degeneration of neurons starts in the temporal lobes of the brain, which are the parts on either side of your head (think: near the temples) that primarily control language and memory functioning. Alzheimer's disease also attacks a structure in the brain called the hippocampus, which lies within the temporal lobe. The hippocampus has nothing to do with hippos. It's shaped a bit like a seahorse, which is why it's named after the Greek word for one—creative, right? The hippocampus is extraordinarily important because it helps us transfer our memories from short-term to long-term storage. It's the part of our brain that helps us make new memories. Many of the memories you have retained throughout your life have been made possible by the hippocampus. So, let's put this together. We have a disease that causes degeneration of the neurons in our temporal lobes (language) and our hippocampus (making new memories). As you might guess, that leads to major impairment in both memory and language functioning.

Language is the area most people don't really think about in Alzheimer's disease, so let's elaborate on that a bit. The main language issue in individuals with Alzheimer's disease is difficulty finding the right word to say in conversation. Just as we mentioned in the section on warning signs, these word-finding issues are not the benign ones that happen to most people every so often. They are frequent, and they are more severe. For example, in our practice we have seen an American man with a Ph.D. in his field who could not name a picture of a lion. Obviously, a well-educated person in contemporary American culture should have absolutely no problem labelling a lion. In this case, the man could not come up with the word, even given hints, and he claimed that he never knew what the creature was called (highly unlikely).

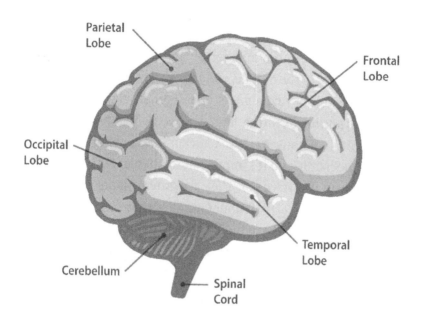

Aphasia is the term used to describe difficulty with language functioning. People with Alzheimer's disease can have both expressive aphasia (trouble verbally expressing themselves) and receptive aphasia (trouble understanding language). Someone with expressive aphasia may have significant word-finding trouble or use words that don't quite make sense given the context of the conversation. They may even use paraphasias, which are errors in speech that are similar to the target word yet still incorrect. For example, someone might say "feet" when they meant to say "days," or "sacrificial" when they meant to say "superficial." Individuals with receptive aphasia can understand bits and pieces of what is said to them, or they might completely misinterpret statements from other people. An example from our practice is an individual who checked their bank account and was told that they had $5,000, only to become upset because they thought they were told that they *owed* $5000 to the bank. Both types of language difficulty can be caused by the damage to the temporal lobes caused by Alzheimer's disease.

There are a few different models that try to describe the different stages of Alzheimer's. Some will split it into seven stages and others will split it into three. For the most part, the number of stages is arbitrary. We prefer to look at it in terms of early, middle, and late stages. A good rule of thumb is that the progression of Alzheimer's is essentially the reverse of normal development from birth. In the later stages, people begin to lose many skills and their functioning starts to look similar to children or babies. We don't mean to be harsh, and it's important to not treat these individuals as if they are children. They are not. They are grown adults who have earned respect over their long life. BUT, understanding that their development has brought them to a place where their thinking and behavior are similar to that of a child can help you approach situations the right way.

The early stages of Alzheimer's disease are characterized by a difficulty with orientation, memory problems, irritability, and minor language impairment. As a reminder, orientation just refers to your awareness of yourself, where you are physically and in time, and the reason for the current circumstances. Basically, how "with it" you are. So, people with early stage Alzheimer's disease will often seem a little "off" due to their difficulties with orientation. They might remember their name and date of birth, but have trouble remembering their phone number or address. They might also begin to lose their sense of time and have trouble when asked to state the day of the week or month of the year.

Recall that Alzheimer's disease affects the hippocampus, which means that these people will have difficulty forming new memories. That means that, in the early stages of the disease, they will likely have little trouble recalling information from their childhood or facts about their field of work that are stored deep within their long-term memory. Common examples of recent memory issues include forgetting recent conversations, not remembering whether a bill has been paid (which can lead to unpaid or double-paid bills), forgetting upcoming appointments, or having difficulty sticking with the narrative of a television show or novel across multiple days.

Irritability in Alzheimer's is fairly straightforward and typically presents as the person being a little quicker to anger or more ornery than usual. You might think of this irritability as the precursor to some of the more depressive elements that emerge when the person starts to become more isolated and sedentary. Language impairment in early Alzheimer's disease usually takes the form of minor word-finding difficulties or mild difficulty with communicating spoken ideas clearly.

Someone in these early stages is likely to still be mostly independent and able to participate meaningfully in their day to day activities. By "meaningfully" we mean they can actively contribute ideas to conversations, play an active role in planning activities, and help with decision making. To clarify, taking your loved one to church and dropping them off, only for them to stare off into space and avoid interacting with their peers, would not count as meaningful participation. We say this because we sometimes see families in our practice who claim their loved one is still very social and has many different weekly activities, only for us to find out that they are essentially being dragged from place to place and not actually participating.

Individuals in the early stages of the disease also benefit well from routines. As long as they are in their usual place and have some typical structure to their daily activities, strangers or acquaintances may not even notice that the person has some cognitive impairment. However, taking this person from their routine and normal environment, as you might when going on a vacation, can highlight their areas of impairment and cause their level of independent functioning to dip a bit. It is often right after a vacation or the holidays that a person is brought in to our office by their family member because they noticed "something was off."

From there the disease progresses into a more readily identifiable form. In the middle stages of Alzheimer's, people begin to have much more significant language problems. They might only be able to effectively communicate with caretakers or loved ones due to issues with aphasia. The slight problems with orientation in the early stages tend to progress into full blown confusion here as well. Rather than seem slightly "off," people in the middle stages of Alzheimer's disease might not understand why they are in a given location such as the doctor's office or demonstrate some major mix ups in the details of a story they're telling. Confabulation is also common during this stage. Confabulation is essentially when there are gaps in the person's memory or awareness and their brain automatically tries to fill them in. This can look like making up stories or combining elements of different events. Families often think the person is lying or just pretending, when the person's brain is actually trying to compensate for the cognitive decline.

It's at this stage that family members and caretakers should be on the lookout for wandering. Say you drop your loved one off at a doctor's office for a routine appointment and they are in the middle stages of Alzheimer's disease. They might be confused about why they're in the office in the first place or not understand exactly where they are. Combine this with worsening memory difficulties and they might assume that they are already done with their appointment and walk out of the building aimlessly. Not good.

Wandering can sometimes be benign and only lead to a front desk worker needing to redirect someone. However, we have recently seen a case that involved an elderly man walking about 20 miles, thinking that he was on his way home. The memory impairment caused by Alzheimer's disease caused him to forget how long he had been walking or why. This led to dehydration, heat stroke, and eventually being picked up by the police off the side of the road. The purpose of this story is not to scare you. It's to illustrate the importance of understanding your loved one's behaviors and level of impairment.

Tips for Managing Wandering:
- Keep a routine and structure for your loved one's day so they're not left bored and directionless.

- Identify most likely times for wandering to occur and schedule activities during those times.

- Exercise and activities can help reduce the agitation and restlessness that might cause someone to wander.

- Reassure your loved one if they express feeling disoriented, lost, or unsure why they are not at home, work, etc.

- Ensure basic needs such as food, rest, and toileting are met.

- Install additional door locks above or below the person's line of sight.

- Use a video doorbell and monitor it throughout the day to keep track of who is entering and leaving the house.
  - WARNING: Video monitoring systems should not be used instead of actual caregivers. As dementia progresses people may need reminders to eat and use the toilet, among other issues. Socialization with others is also an important component of everyone's life.

- Use a device such as a bell or home alarm system to notify when a door or window has been opened.

- Place car keys out of sight if they are not driving anymore.

Regarding memory, at this point the person may not only be having trouble recalling recent information, but also show some impairment in their ability to remember more deeply stored information. For example, they may forget what their main career was throughout their life or struggle to remember the names of family members.

As we mentioned, Alzheimer's disease begins in the temporal lobes and the hippocampus, but during the middle stages, the degeneration spreads to other areas of the brain. Specifically, you might see some impairment of the frontal lobes, which manage higher-order thinking skills like planning and decision making. Therefore, this person is likely going to have much more trouble trying to solve problems, following multiple-step instructions, or coming to a decision. This can lead to a sort of paralysis when faced with something as simple as deciding where they would like to eat or what to get someone as a birthday gift. They may also have trouble following a sequence that used to come easily, such as cooking from a recipe or engaging in a hobby like knitting.

During this stage you also might get a new symptom called "apraxia." Apraxia refers to the inability to carry out pre-programmed or well-rehearsed motor tasks. The first functions to go are more complicated ones, such as job-related tasks or tasks involving newer technology. Eventually, they may even have difficulty carrying out basic daily living tasks such as brushing their teeth or dressing themselves. To be clear, apraxia does not refer to difficulty with motor tasks due to pain, fatigue, or a movement disorder such as Parkinson's disease. Rather, this is an impairment in the part of the brain used to carry out these common motor functions. As you might infer from the increased confusion and difficulty carrying out tasks of daily living, people in the middle stages of Alzheimer's disease tend to become much more dependent on others. They may be able to live with some degree of independence if they are monitored closely and given ample support, but they are typically unable to safely live on their own.

The later stages of Alzheimer's disease are not pretty. Hopefully, at some point in time this section of the book will become irrelevant due to breakthrough advances in medicine. For now, there is no cure for Alzheimer's and it typically ends with the individual's death. As of 2016, the typical course of Alzheimer's takes about 10 years. After that, the person dies due to "complications." When you hear a doctor or the media refer to "complications due to Alzheimer's," what they mean is that the person's cognitive and physical state is so poor that they are no longer able to survive.

In the later stages of Alzheimer's disease, normal bodily functions become impaired. The most common cause of death in people with advanced Alzheimer's disease is pneumonia due to difficulties swallowing properly. People in this stage also experience significant difficulties with basic skills such as walking, speaking, and even remembering to eat. All of these contribute to an overall frailty that makes even slight illnesses or infections devastating to the individual.

People with late-stage Alzheimer's dementia will have difficulty expressing themselves with language. Therefore, a minor infection can exist for an extended period and become much more severe because the person isn't able to express their discomfort. As you may imagine, individuals with late-stage Alzheimer's are completely dependent on other people. They typically need 24-hour care from family members or support staff. Often these individuals live in an intensive care facility where trained staff support their needs. Another option that many families choose is called hospice. Hospice is also known as "end of life" care and is typically advised for individuals that have a prognosis of less than six months to live. Hospice care is focused on providing comfort for the individual during their final months and can often be organized within the home.

One last stage to mention here is called "preclinical" Alzheimer's disease, which comes before all the other stages that we have described so far. This is a new stage that has been recognized in recent years. Essentially, due to a better understanding of the pathology associated with Alzheimer's, doctors can now identify the disease in the brain years before it has any detectable effect on functioning. They do this through imaging techniques that allow them to look at buildup of amyloid plaque or other evidence of problems with the neurons in the brain. Right now, these assessments are mostly used for clinical or drug research.

Alzheimer's Disease Stages	
Preclinical Alzheimer's Disease	Noticeable brain changes that indicate the possible presence of Alzheimer's disease with no significant cognitive problems yet.
Early Stage Alzheimer's Disease (Mild)	Person is likely still independent. Short term memory difficulties and word finding trouble present.
Middle Stage Alzheimer's Disease (Moderate)	Usually the longest stage. Pronounced memory difficulties including long-term/ autobiographical memory. Behavioral changes and generalized confusion.
Late Stage Alzheimer's Disease (Severe)	Fully dependent on others. Loss of awareness of surroundings. Changes in physical abilities. Severe difficulty communicating. Increased risk of infections.

As noted earlier in our discussion of Mild Cognitive Impairment, the hope is that treatments might be developed that can stop Alzheimer's in this earliest stage before it is causing a person any impairment. The field of research into Alzheimer's disease treatment and prevention is moving rapidly. With increased understanding of the biomarkers and genetics that are linked to Alzheimer's disease, it is our hope that treatment and prevention options will soon be available. Even though there are currently no long-term solutions to Alzheimer's disease, accurate diagnosis is important, especially in the early stages. The disease is going to progress no matter what, but there are currently treatments that can delay the impairment and improve quality of life for the individual. It is also extremely important to understand whether the cause of the person's decline is Alzheimer's disease or whether there may be another, potentially less devastating, culprit. The diagnosis process typically involves several stages and can honestly be somewhat confusing, especially if you've never been through it before. Fortunately, the process for obtaining a comprehensive diagnosis is similar for each of the different issues that we will cover in this book. In a later chapter we cover the entire diagnosis procedure, including which doctors you will work with and what sort of testing and evaluation is usually required.

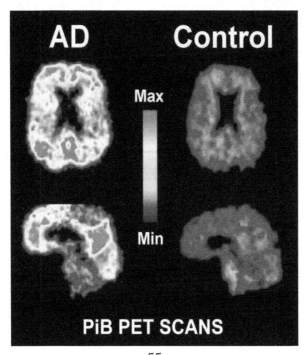

In the case of dementia caused by Alzheimer's disease, it will typically involve a short screening for cognitive problems done by a doctor, then more extensive testing by a neuropsychologist. After testing of thinking skills is complete, the diagnosis will be confirmed by brain imaging. For Alzheimer's disease, this is often done with a PET scan in addition to MRI imaging. PET refers to Positron Emission Tomography, which uses a (harmless) radioactive chemical compound, called a tracer, to reveal how the tissues in your brain are functioning.

Alzheimer's Disease:
- A "neurodegenerative" disease that causes the cells in the brain to progressively break down.
- Typically starts in the areas of the brain associated with memory and language.
- Eventually spreads to affect other parts of the brain.
- Involves beta-amyloid plaques and neurofibrillary tangles that disrupt the functioning of neurons in the brain.
- Early stages characterized by short-term memory difficulties and minor disorientation.
- Later stages involve significant memory loss, trouble communicating, and behavior changes.
- There is no current cure or effective treatment to slow the progression of the illness.
- People with Alzheimer's disease inevitably deteriorate in their thinking abilities to the point that they would be considered to have dementia.

The older, and more common, version of this test is called the FDG-PET scan. The FDG part refers to fluorodeoxyglucose (you don't need to remember these names), which is the particular radioactive tracer used in this version of the scan. Tracking the movement of FDG around the brain gives a better idea about which areas are using the most energy in the form of sugar. This older type of PET scan is helpful for many purposes, such as diagnosing cancer or problems with blood flow, but there is a newer type of scan that's more useful in diagnosing Alzheimer's disease.

As of the writing of this book, the most accurate imaging technique for Alzheimer's is called a PiB PET scan or amyloid PET scan, which uses a tracer called Pittsburgh Compound B (developed at University of Pittsburgh). This tracer is super useful in the case of detecting Alzheimer's because it binds to those nasty beta-amyloid plaques that build up in your brain as your neurons start to degenerate. Basically, it can more accurately show the wreckage of Alzheimer's disease on your brain cells. As we mentioned, the only definitive way to look at the impact of beta-amyloid in the brain is through an autopsy. A PiB PET scan helps us get pretty close and is possible while the person is still alive, which is why it is becoming an essential part of the diagnosis process along with other medical evidence and testing results.

Frontotemporal Degeneration

Now that we have covered some particulars about Alzheimer's disease, let's look at another form of cortical dementia caused by frontotemporal lobar degeneration (or FTD). Dementia caused by frontotemporal degeneration is less common than that caused by Alzheimer's disease, accounting for somewhere between 5 and 10 percent of dementia cases. It generally has an earlier age of onset and is most commonly diagnosed between 45 and 64 years old. Where Alzheimer's disease started off with degeneration of neurons in the temporal lobes (sides of the brain), frontotemporal degeneration starts in the frontal lobe. Your frontal lobe sits right behind your forehead and controls a lot of really important functions. In fact, a large frontal lobe is one of the evolutionary advantages of human beings. If you look at lower organisms, they have very small frontal lobes. That's because the frontal lobe of the brain influences your personality and behaviors, as well as "higher order" thinking skills like multitasking, planning, visualizing outcomes, and manipulating information in your mind. You may hear the term "executive functioning" to describe the role of the frontal lobe, since these higher order skills essentially manage and exhibit control over your other thinking processes. Remember that cortical dementias affect that outer bark of the brain rather than the underlying connections. That means frontotemporal degeneration directly impacts the skills we're describing here.

Overall, frontotemporal degeneration progresses very similarly to Alzheimer's disease except that it begins in a different area within the brain. Since Alzheimer's starts in the temporal lobes, the first symptoms are language and memory impairment. With frontotemporal degeneration, since it begins in the frontal lobe, the first symptoms usually have to do with behavior or personality. We're going to cover one particular variant of the disease here, which is the behavioral variant. There are a few others, but they may be beyond the scope of this book. One of the most disturbing symptoms of frontotemporal degeneration is behavioral disinhibition, or the inability to appropriately control behavior. In a normally functioning person, someone might have unfortunate private thoughts such as "Man, that person is ugly!" or "I wish this guy would just shut up!", but you would typically never say those out loud because you understand it would be inappropriate. Someone who is developing frontotemporal degeneration might lose some of that ability to inhibit (hold back) their behavior and end up blurting out inappropriate or embarrassing statements.

Just like all the memory issues we talked about in the Alzheimer's section, it is essential to remember that you are looking for a change from the person's previous functioning. If your loved one has always said exactly what is on their mind and has gotten in trouble throughout their entire life for never having a filter, you wouldn't necessarily take their odd behavior as evidence of dementia. That's just them being their typical strange self. What we often see in clinical practice is clearer and more pronounced. For instance, we have seen 80-year-old women who have been polite and kind throughout their life begin to make inappropriate comments to people in the line at a store or walk around naked when there are visitors in the home. These are not malicious behaviors or even intentional attempts to be silly. This is their frontal lobe losing the ability to regulate their behavior. People with this sort of disinhibition typically don't understand that their behavior is inappropriate. This can be a very tough sort of dementia to deal with because these behavioral symptoms can come before any difficulty with memory or other thinking skills are apparent. Therefore, there is no other obvious evidence that something is actually wrong with their brain. Many families end up distancing themselves from the person because they are offensive or act in ways that are not appropriate around children.

Aside from disinhibition and a lack of "mental filter," you might see full-on personality changes. In general, we expect someone's basic personality to stay mostly constant across their lifetime. Common personality factors include how agreeable and easygoing someone is, how outgoing and extroverted they are, and how neurotic and preoccupied they are. With frontotemporal degeneration you may begin to see slight changes or a complete flipping of someone's personality. For example, someone who has characteristically been outgoing, gregarious, and loving throughout their entire life might start to become grumpy around people and prefer to be left alone.

Of course, a certain degree of this could be attributed to age, as we all begin to develop different priorities as time goes on. However, you typically wouldn't expect someone who is primarily extroverted to suddenly become a huge introvert and avoid interaction with other people. Likewise, you might see an individual who has always been a miserly grump suddenly become very affectionate and loving. If you find yourself thinking your loved one is just not the person you remember, ask yourself if what you are seeing is a change in their core personality. As with any dementia symptom, this particular quirk would not prove that the person has frontotemporal degeneration in and of itself. Instead, it's one extra piece of evidence that can, along with other information, help you identify what exactly is going on.

In addition to the more obvious symptoms of disinhibition and changes to personality we've described, frontotemporal degeneration can feature some more subtle signs and symptoms you should be aware of. A really interesting symptom that often surprises families we work with is diet and appetite changes. Changes in eating behaviors are sometimes an early symptom of frontotemporal degeneration. In particular, these people tend to overeat and consume high-sugar foods. We sometimes see families who will bring in their loved one for assessment and express concerns over finding piles of candy wrappers, chips, and other junk food around their home. This is confusing for the family because they have characteristically had more self-control. While this symptom is relatively subtle, it can be important in elderly populations where there is a high rate of cardiovascular disease or diabetes. Typically, a person with frontotemporal degeneration will have limited insight into the fact that their eating behaviors have changed significantly. They are aware they eat snacks but may not know that this is different than their previous behavior, and that they might be going overboard with the snacks. This is thought to be due to degeneration within a complex network of brain structures in this form of dementia, rather than just decreased judgment regarding food. In some related forms of dementia that are a little too nuanced to bore you with here, the person becomes more rigid in their preferences and only wants to eat one type of food. Overall, if you notice a distinct shift in dietary preferences or eating behaviors in your loved one that doesn't strike you as normal, it may be worth having them checked out.

A person with frontotemporal degeneration might also experience changes in their behaviors related to personal hygiene. You may notice that the person smells worse than they normally do, has unkempt clothing, has inappropriately grown-out nails, or has stopped caring for their teeth or dentures. As with the changes in diet, the person will likely have poor insight into their unusual behavior. Families of people with frontotemporal degeneration often complain that they need to practically force their loved one to take showers or bathe. This can occur in Alzheimer's disease as well, but that is typically more related to the person forgetting whether they already bathed. In the case of frontotemporal degeneration, the person just does not feel the imperative to bathe that normally functioning individuals do. This is another reason that frontotemporal degeneration is often quite hard for families to live with. You have a person who is beginning to behave inappropriately, perhaps becoming unpleasant, and they are also difficult to be around due to persistently poor hygiene. Family involvement is often important to help these people establish simple and consistent routines to compensate for their lack of awareness around hygiene.

Some interesting emotional symptoms can also occur in frontotemporal degeneration. Aside from the strange behavioral symptoms of becoming inappropriate or disinhibited, a person with frontotemporal degeneration can develop emotional symptoms that look a lot like depression. If you care for someone with this disease you may find it becomes very difficult to motivate them and get them moving. Maybe they used to stay active by participating in community events, exercising, and meeting up with friends for meals, but now they can hardly be bothered to leave the house for an important event like a family birthday. They might seem to become quite apathetic and uninterested in things they used to be passionate about.

Along with this, you can sometimes see blunting of emotions, which means they express a narrower range of emotion overall. You may become upset and cry when you hear bad news, or you may scream with excitement when your team wins the Superbowl. In some people with frontotemporal degeneration, their emotional range is much smaller. They might grin slightly when meeting a new grandchild, whereas they would previously be completely elated. In other cases, they may express very little outward emotion even when a longtime friend passes away. These emotional changes are not deliberate attempts to be cruel. Emotional functioning is largely centered in the frontal lobe of the brain and unfortunately that's exactly the area that is beginning to break down with this disease.

As mentioned, the frontal lobe manages the group of skills called executive functions. That means that many more complex thinking skills involved in the business of being a modern human will be impacted by frontotemporal degeneration. Therefore, someone with frontotemporal degeneration may begin to show significant difficulty in everyday situations. For instance, if you take them to a restaurant, they may have a hard time deciding what they would like to eat. They might also have trouble following along with the conversation at the table due to their difficulty in processing multiple pieces of information at once. For this person, it might be overwhelming to be expected to read a menu, listen to conversation, and contribute thoughtfully all at the same time.

At home, you may notice they have become much more disorganized. Whereas they used to keep their affairs in decent order, now they have piles of unopened mail and are not using a calendar effectively. It's not uncommon to see a great number of yellow sticky notes on someone's desk or refrigerator to remind them of upcoming events or important to-dos. However, they might have so many notes to themselves that they can't remember which ones are new and which ones are old. They will also likely have a hard time planning ahead. If you ask them to accomplish several tasks that have a logical order, they may mix up the order or leave steps out entirely.

A good example of this is people who have characteristically done the cooking in their household for many years and then begin to have trouble following recipes. In this instance they might accidentally forget to put water in a pot before turning on the stove or completely burn something while preparing the side dishes. As with all the other symptoms presented in this section, this must be a change. My brother-in-law (Dr. Duff speaking) is over 30 and this is pretty much his standard. He couldn't make spaghetti to save his life, so this behavior would be pretty normal for him. However, if my wife, who is an amazing cook, began to behave this way, I would be quite worried.

Alzheimer's Disease	Frontotemporal Degeneration
Progressive degeneration of the brain.	Progressive degeneration of the brain.
Starts in temporal lobes and spreads from there.	Starts in frontal lobe and spreads from there.
Initial difficulty is short term memory loss.	Initial difficulty is behavioral change and disorganization.
Late stages are characterized by global impairment and loss of basic functions.	Late stages are characterized by global impairment and loss of basic functions.

To close out this section on frontotemporal degeneration, we must remind you that this is a progressive disorder just like Alzheimer's disease. The brain will continue to gradually deteriorate over time. While that process continues, the degeneration will spread and affect other areas of the brain. This means that, while memory is not a primary complaint early on in frontotemporal degeneration, eventually the person can have deficits there. Same goes for other skills such as visuospatial functioning and language. The course of the disorder is a little different than Alzheimer's disease. The age of onset is a little earlier, typically between 45 and 65. Research on this disorder is constantly evolving, but the current literature suggests there is a genetic component. In other words, if you have a parent with the disease, you are more likely to develop it. Interestingly, the genetic link appears to be stronger for frontotemporal degeneration than it does for Alzheimer's.

The life expectancy for people with frontotemporal degeneration varies depending on the individual and which particular subtype you're looking at (we didn't cover the subtypes here because that is more detail than you need to know right now). In general, the average life expectancy for someone with frontotemporal degeneration is 7 to 13 years. In the later stages of the disease, the person will look a lot like a late-stage Alzheimer's patient (global dementia). They will need 24-hour care and help moving around since they'll begin to lose coordination of their muscles. Eventually basic functions like swallowing and controlling their bladder or bowels begin to break down. It is usually complications caused by these deficits in basic functions that lead to death.

Case Study – Frontotemporal Dementia

Howard is an 80-year-old man who retired from the United States Marine Corps after a full career of military service. Throughout his life, he was known by his family and friends as a stoic man of few words who was always polite but would never be described as a social butterfly.

In recent years, family members have started to notice a distinct change in his personality. While he has always been a quiet, introspective man, Howard is now outgoing and gregarious. He will frequently talk to strangers on the sidewalk or in stores, sometimes for an excessively long time. Howard will also sometimes share information with strangers that most people would find inappropriate such as stories about people he killed in his military service or his pornography habits.

Unlike his history of being even-tempered, Howard has recently had trouble controlling his anger, snapping at family members and strangers over minor issues. As a result, Howard's family has started to distance themselves from him. Howard's daughter has stopped bringing her family over for the holidays after he called his granddaughter a "stupid little twerp." Spending any time with Howard also makes it clear that he is not appropriately bathing and grooming himself. His wife complains that it is "like pulling teeth" to make him take a shower, and she often elects to let him have poor hygiene rather than endure his angry outbursts.

From Howard's point of view, he has no issues and feels that everyone else is making a big deal out of nothing. He often brings up his military service and insinuates his family should have more respect for someone that has sacrificed so much for the good of his country.

We will discuss more about how to diagnose and treat frontotemporal degeneration in a later chapter. For now, you should recognize that it is a progressive disease that we have no way of stopping at the moment, and treatment mainly focuses on reducing the impact of the symptoms we described in this section.

Lewy Body Disease

Now onto a really interesting one! In this section we are going to talk about dementia caused by Lewy body disease. For a long time, this is one that most people had never heard of. In recent years, however, the disease has gained recognition due to the fact that after Robin Williams' suicide, the autopsy indicated he was likely suffering from Lewy body disease. A simple way of thinking about Lewy body disease is that it looks like a combination of Alzheimer's disease (which we have covered) and Parkinson's disease (which we will cover shortly). So far, we have generally been splitting the different forms of dementia up into cortical and subcortical types, but this one kind of falls in between, as it affects both the outer cortex of the brain as well as the internal connections between the different lobes (subcortical).

So why is it called Lewy body disease? It's actually pretty simple. In 1942, this German neurologist named Frederic Lewy discovered abnormal clumps of protein in the brain that lead to a variety of symptoms we will cover in this section, and he decided to name these clumps after himself: Lewy bodies. We must occasionally remind family members that Lewy did not "invent" Lewy bodies, he just discovered them and gave them a name, therefore any resentment toward him is a bit misplaced. Technically speaking, Lewy bodies are abnormal deposits of a protein called alpha-synuclein. This protein normally helps the neurons in your brain communicate with one another by helping to push neurotransmitters (chemical messengers) out into the synapse (space between neurons). When the protein becomes clumped together into these Lewy bodies, it can cause a variety of interesting and troubling difficulties for the person.

Basically, Lewy body disease causes three core symptoms: fluctuations in cognitive abilities, movement symptoms, and visual hallucinations. Let's talk about visual hallucinations first because that can be one of the most confusing and scary symptoms for both the person suffering from the disease as well as their family or caregivers. The term hallucination simply refers to perceiving something with your senses that is not actually there. The most common hallucinations are visual (seeing something that isn't there) or auditory (hearing something no one else hears). Hallucinations can also happen with other sorts of dementias. In these cases, they're usually due to the brain trying to use a shortcut to fill in information that isn't actually there, because it is no longer processing information the way it used to.

In the case of Lewy body disease, the cause is a bit different and the hallucinations are typically of a different type than those caused by other types of dementia. With the non-Lewy body hallucinations, the person will often see an object and mistake it for something else. For example, in clinical practice we have seen individuals who see a purse on the counter and think it's a cat, or people who have striped sheets and think they see snakes on their bed. In Lewy body disease, hallucinations can also seem to happen without any external prompt. They may have some basis in reality, such as seeing a shadow and thinking there's someone walking around, but they can also happen regardless of the situation. Interestingly, one of the most common hallucinations for people with Lewy body disease is seeing small, human-like figures in the room. Some examples we have heard are children, little people, Oompa Loompas, elves, or goblins running across the room. Seeing small animals is also common.

With Lewy body disease, the hallucinations are not always visual, but they seem to be the most common. As opposed to hallucinations you might get from other disorders, these ones are what we'd call "well formed," meaning they aren't just a vague shape or essence. They actually look real to the person. These hallucinations may or may not cause fear, so sometimes they go unnoticed for quite some time because the person doesn't bother to tell anyone about them. In other cases, they can be quite pronounced and scary. We saw someone in clinical practice a few years ago who thought there was a parade of small Native American people in traditional headdresses that would go through her house or down the street at night. This was very upsetting to her. That about covers what you need to know about hallucinations in Lewy body disease. They are most often well-formed visual hallucinations. Often, they are of kids or little people.

The next defining characteristic of Lewy body disease is fluctuation in cognition and mental status. This is usually one of the key points of information that helps us clinicians recognize we might be dealing with Lewy body disease rather than Alzheimer's or some other cause of dementia. When we say "fluctuations" we basically mean that the person suffering from this disease has good days and bad days. More than that, there is a clear and significant difference between the good days and the bad days. On a good day, it can even seem as if they are nearly their normal selves, while at other times they may seem very confused and impaired in their thinking abilities. While we said "good days and bad days" the fluctuations can vary in duration, sometimes lasting just a few hours and sometimes lasting several days. This can cause some uninformed families to think their loved one is "faking it" or just trying to be difficult, since they are seemingly able. This is not the case. The person has no control over these cognitive fluctuations. For example, a person who is suffering from Lewy body disease may seem nearly normal on one day. They are able to answer basic questions about where they would like to go for lunch, they're aware they have medication to take, and they seem to understand their surroundings and the people who are with them. When they have a fluctuation and experience a decline in their mental status, they might appear very confused. They may be disoriented and unsure of where they are at a given moment. They might also have a difficult time understanding instructions or participating in decision making. The difference between these moments of clarity and moments of confusion can be startling for some individuals. In our clinical practice, we have seen individuals who are significantly impaired during our time with them. But their family tells us that they seem well enough to get behind the wheel of a car at other times.

The final core symptom of Lewy body disease that we will talk about here is what we in the field would call "parkinsonism." That just means the person has motor difficulties (issues with their movement) that mirror those experienced in Parkinson's disease. We'll talk more about Parkinson's later on, as that is another disease that can lead to dementia in some individuals. However, for now you should know that Parkinson's disease is a movement disorder that can cause a variety of issues with motor functioning.

In Parkinson's disease, some of the most common motor symptoms are tremor, balance problems, worsening posture, and difficulty with one's gait (walking ability). In someone with Lewy body disease, similar movement issues are frequently present. If the movement difficulties are not as severe as you would see in someone with full-blown Parkinson's, you might hear the term "mild parkinsonism" used. The most common parkinsonian symptoms in someone with Lewy body disease would be stooped posture, lack of balance, smaller handwriting, a tremor (rhythmic shaking movement), shuffling steps, and slowed movement. These symptoms are by no means consistent. Between different people with Lewy body disease, the parkinsonian movement symptoms can vary. These are just a few things to look out for.

Interestingly, these movement symptoms can also fluctuate along with the cognitive skills. On one day the person may enjoy walking around the neighborhood as a typical leisure activity. The next day, they may seem to have immense difficulty walking and get lost in their own neighborhood. These motor symptoms can be startling and frustrating for families. It's not uncommon for a family to bring their loved one on a trip when they appear to be their normal, well-functioning self only for them to be wracked with confusion and movement difficulties on the second day. While it takes several professionals to accurately diagnose Lewy body disease, your awareness of these cardinal symptoms of fluctuating cognitive abilities, motor problems, and visual hallucinations can definitely help point healthcare providers in the right direction. The person does not need to have every symptom to be diagnosed with the disorder. They can be free of hallucinations, or have no motor difficulties, and still have Lewy body disease.

Lewy Body Disease
- Progressive brain disease involving abnormal clumps of protein called Lewy bodies.
- Causes a unique combination of symptoms including:
  o Parkinson's-like movement difficulties.
  o Visual hallucinations.
  o Cognitive impairment.
  o Significant fluctuation in severity of symptoms day to day.

Finally, we should talk a bit about the progression of Lewy body disease. Unfortunately, like Alzheimer's disease, Lewy body disease is a progressive disease in which the person inevitably continues declining over time. Like

Alzheimer's, the disease typically takes hold in the later 60s, though there are some cases in which it begins earlier.

Unlike Alzheimer's disease, which has fairly consistent stages of progression, Lewy body disease is far less predictable. It's therefore difficult to give a standard rate of progression. On average the disease runs its course in about 8 years, but this should not be used as a firm guideline since the timeline can vary from 2 to 20 years! In the future there very well may be new forms of identification and diagnosis that can give a better idea of a particular person's prognosis and what the course of their disease will look like, but unfortunately that time is not now.

Creutzfeldt-Jakob Disease

Though it's not as present in the news these days, you're probably familiar with the term "mad cow disease." Basically, it's a neurodegenerative disease (breaks down neurons in the brain) that occurs in cows. In cows, the disease is caused by something called a prion, which is basically a misfolded protein that becomes an infectious agent. Certain prions can spread to other proteins, functioning similarly to a viral infection. The unfortunate thing about mad cow disease (technically known as bovine spongiform encephalopathy) is that it can spread from cows to humans. When a human ingests contaminated meat or food that has accidentally been in contact with infected carcasses, the person will acquire the disease. Once it spreads to a human, it becomes known as Creutzfeldt-Jakob disease (CJD). Technically this type of CJD acquired through mad cow disease is just one particular variant of several. The issues caused by CJD are a bit more hardcore than many other forms of dementia. The disease causes tissue within the brain to break down rapidly and develop tiny holes, giving it a sponge-like appearance. CJD is considered to be incurable and universally fatal, meaning there is no way to stop the progression and it invariably leads to death, often in just a year or two. The reason we are mentioning mad cow disease and the associated Creutzfeldt-Jakob disease is that's a much less common disease that can also cause dementia. Within a few months, the affected person can experience personality changes, emotional symptoms such as anxiety or depression, memory loss, difficulty speaking, and other impaired thinking abilities. While it is relatively unlikely that you will run into someone who has dementia from CJD, it's here as a reminder that there are many different disorders, including rare ones, that can cause dementia.

Subcortical Dementias

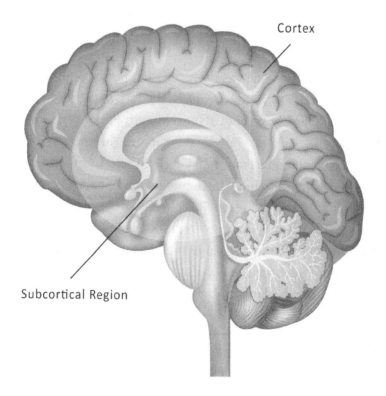

Cortex

Subcortical Region

Now we're going to switch gears a bit. So far in this section, we have been talking about cortical dementias, or dementias that affect the outer bark of the brain. For the next part, we're going to focus on the other side of the coin: subcortical dementias. You may be able to guess what "subcortical" means: the stuff going on beneath the cortex. Rather than housing the big overall skills such as memory, language, or vision, the subcortical space involves more basic functions like reflexes. Most importantly, this is where the various parts of the brain connect with one another. Therefore, rather than affecting the major thinking skills, subcortical dementias have a bigger impact on the efficiency with which someone can use those skills. Instead of outright difficulties with memory or language, you are more likely to see difficulty with attention and concentration, or decreased speed of thinking. The main subcortical dementias that we'd like to introduce you to in this section are those caused by Parkinson's disease and Huntington's disease.

Parkinson's Disease

Let's start with Parkinson's disease, which is the more common one. You may be familiar with its physical effects. Legendary boxer Muhammad Ali and actor Michael J. Fox have both struggled with Parkinson's conditions in the public eye. The primary physical symptoms are mostly related to movement and can include tremor (shaking) of limbs or other body parts; slowed movement and difficulty starting movement; balance and posture issues; and difficulties walking. In Parkinson's disease, the subcortical regions in your brain that are responsible for creating the neurotransmitter dopamine break down and stop functioning normally. This has a major effect, because dopamine plays an essential role in regulating movement and coordination.

Parkinson's is a progressive disease. We have some decent medications to treat the motor symptoms of Parkinson's disease, such as the carbidopa/levodopa combination. These drugs help increase the production of dopamine in those crucial subcortical regions in the brain, effectively counteracting the effects of the disease. Treatment of motor symptoms can actually improve the overall course of the disease. Untreated, most people will become bed bound and unable to move effectively within 10 years. Current medication treatments can prolong that for five years or more. However, it's a bit hard to speak generally about the course of Parkinson's because it can vary quite a bit between individuals.

Parkinson's Disease Physical Symptoms:
- -Tremor
- -Balance Problems
- -Stooped Posture
- -Shuffling Gait
- -Motor "Freezing"
- -Slowness
- -Muscle Rigidity

So, what does this movement condition have to do with dementia? It turns out that about half of people who have Parkinson's disease will go on to experience thinking difficulties that qualify them for a diagnosis of dementia. Since the changes that come along with Parkinson's are subcortical in nature, the cognitive impairment looks a bit different than it does for the cortical dementias like Alzheimer's disease or frontotemporal degeneration. Someone with dementia caused by Parkinson's disease can also have problems with their memory, but the memory difficulties follow a different pattern from Alzheimer's. People with Alzheimer's experience rapid forgetting of new information. If you have a conversation with them, they may not remember it the next day. Not just the details of what you talked about, but they may not remember ever having the conversation in the first place. Their brain is not properly storing the information. With Parkinson's disease, the thinking difficulties mimic the physical changes that occur. Rather than losing memory, people with Parkinson's can have their thinking skills become slower and less efficient.

The process of memory is broken up into several stages. Learning/encoding is the process through which you write new memories into your brain. Storage is your brain's ability to hold that information. Retrieval is how well you're able to pull those memories out when you want them.

In Alzheimer's, you will see issues with learning, where the person is less able to write new memories. If they're able to learn some information, their impaired storage means they will not be able to hold onto it for a significant amount of time. That's why they don't remember ever having that conversation just the day before. In Parkinson's disease, you are more likely to see issues with retrieval. The person will be slower in their ability to learn new information, but they can still do it with effort. However, they will have a harder time retrieving that information from their memory storage when they need it. For this reason, cues (hints) can help the person with Parkinson's to remember the information. In this hypothetical situation with the conversation on the previous day, a person with Parkinson's dementia may only faintly remember the event of having a conversation. But when provided with cues such as "Remember? We talked about Jane's birthday plans?" they may be able to pull up some of that stored information from the conversation and recover details from what was discussed. For the person with Alzheimer's disease, these cues and hints would not help them remember. A helpful rule of thumb is that someone with Alzheimer's disease actually loses their memory while someone with cognitive impairment due to Parkinson's loses their ability to use their memory efficiently. It should also be noted that many dementia conditions reach a sort of convergence as they progress into the later stages, where the person is so impaired that it is somewhat difficult (and less useful) to determine the exact type of memory impairment they're having.

Senses perceive information

Attention temporarily holds information

Information is **encoded** for storage

Information is **stored** in memory

Information is **retrieved** when needed

In Parkinson's dementia, language skills are usually still functional. Problems with speed are typically more related to motor difficulties with the muscles involved in speech. For instance, it's common for people with Parkinson's disease to develop a gravelly or hoarse voice and have difficulty controlling their vocal volume. This is due to them losing voluntary control of the muscles in their throat that regulate the process of speech. These problems with the physical aspects of speech should not be confused with that aphasia we talked about before. Someone with Parkinson's should usually still be able to construct coherent sentences and would not have major difficulty understanding what is said to them, although these processes may be a bit slower and more effortful. Having a diminished and unclear voice can be quite frustrating and impair communication, which sometimes leads a person with Parkinson's disease to become less interested in conversing (especially when paired with age-related hearing loss). This sometimes causes a false positive for families in which they think their loved one is losing their language ability. But it's actually just becoming more difficult to interact with others without a great amount of effort, so the person doesn't bother. Given less efficient thinking, you may see the person have trouble thinking of what to say as quickly and clearly as they used to, but they should typically still be able to communicate.

Executive functioning is another category of thinking skills that is often impaired in people with Parkinson's disease. As a reminder, executive functions are those higher-level thinking skills driven mainly by the frontal lobe of the brain. They include things like being able to pay attention in the face of distractions, multitasking, and quickly adapting to changes. When you have impairment in executive functioning, you see a drop in the efficiency and the ease with which a person can access all of their other thinking skills. Maybe they are able to hold a conversation at home, but when they're in a restaurant with many other things competing for their attention, they might have a harder time. A person with Parkinson's dementia might be able to remember how to cook a familiar dish in the kitchen after some reminders from a recipe book but may have a hard time keeping all the steps in sequence and adequately planning their approach to the meal. They may temporarily lose focus on the item boiling on the stove because they're trying to focus on cutting vegetables, whereas they used to be able to keep all of the different steps in mind at once. These difficulties highlight the origin of the term "executive functioning." If you think about a company, the executive's job is not to complete the day-to-day tasks of the workplace, but to coordinate and manage all the people below them to make the process smooth. Executive functioning plays the same role in our brains. The brain of a person with Parkinson's dementia can seem like a busy workplace with no CEO. The workers have not forgotten how to do their jobs, but without someone keeping the process running like a well-oiled machine, productivity slows to a crawl.

The final area of impairment we will mention regarding dementia caused by Parkinson's disease is hallucinations and delusions that are a little different than those seen in a psychiatric disorder like Schizophrenia. In Parkinson's, they are more driven by the brain slowing down as we have described. Evolutionarily, humans have adapted to always be on the lookout for danger. We try to rapidly make sense of our environment, which helped early humans quickly notice a rustling bush in the distance and avoid being mauled by a tiger. Our brains are hardwired to notice patterns and quickly make decisions based on them. This is also why a typically functioning person might see faces or animals in the clouds.

Unfortunately, when the functioning of the brain slows down, as it does in Parkinson's dementia, we can jump to conclusions without processing the necessary information. As a result, a person with Parkinson's dementia might think there are bugs in their home when it's simply the "popcorn" texture on the ceiling, or mistake a purse on the table for a cat. In other cases, they may believe things that aren't true due to this same process of jumping to conclusions without processing all of the information available. It's not rare for a person with Parkinson's dementia to believe someone is stealing from them or become paranoid about the intentions of people in their environment. This is a symptom that sometimes flies under the radar because the person suffering is too embarrassed to bring it up to their families or in doctors' appointments. If your loved one has dementia, help educate them about the fact that these types of symptoms are normal so that they are more likely to clue you in to them. Hallucinations and delusions in Parkinson's disease are often treatable. Sometimes they are exacerbated by dopamine medication, which is used to treat the motor symptoms. In this case, it may simply be a medication adjustment that is called for. Keep the doctor informed!

Parkinson's is a progressive disease, meaning cognitive impairment caused by the disorder tends to get worse over time. As mentioned, not everyone with Parkinson's disease will develop dementia. For those who end up becoming cognitively impaired, it can take several years before they are impaired enough to qualify for a dementia diagnosis. Currently, the estimated average is about 10 years between a diagnosis of Parkinson's and the development of dementia. Since there are many potential causes of Parkinson's disease and different ages of onset, the timeline for progression of dementia caused by the disease varies. On average, death occurs about 8 years after the diagnosis of Parkinson's dementia (not Parkinson's disease itself). As with Alzheimer's, the disease itself doesn't kill the individual, but it causes risk factors for things like pneumonia, choking, or falls that the person may not be able to recover from.

Parkinson's Disease:
- A neurodegenerative disease that causes a breakdown in the areas of the brain that produce dopamine.
- The abnormal dopamine production causes physical difficulties such as:
  - Difficulty with gait (walking).
  - Balance issues.
  - Decreased muscle strength and coordination.
  - Tremor (shaking).
  - Decreased facial expression.
- In some cases, Parkinson's disease causes cognitive difficulties such as slower speed of thinking and poor memory retrieval.
- Physical symptoms can be treated with dopamine-producing medication.

That covers it for what we could call idiopathic Parkinson's, meaning that it appears spontaneously and the source is unknown. About 15 percent of people with Parkinsonism, however, develop an atypical variant called a "Parkinson's plus condition." These are disorders that have regular Parkinson's symptoms with additional symptoms that often do not respond well to normal Parkinson's treatment. We already talked about one Parkinson's plus condition in the section on Lewy body disease. The others include multiple system atrophy (MSA), progressive supranuclear palsy (PSP), and corticobasal degeneration (CBD). For the purposes of this book, we only dive into PSP as a means of giving you the general idea of

Parkinson's plus conditions (they can be complicated and difficult to spot, even for medical providers).

Progressive Supranuclear Palsy

Progressive supranuclear palsy (PSP) is a great example of a Parkinson's plus condition because it highlights how difficult they can be to accurately diagnose. It takes a very attentive group of medical professionals to identify the unique grouping of symptoms that separates it from typical Parkinson's disease. For PSP, one of the clearest differences is that balance problems occur quite early in the disease process. At this stage it's common for people with PSP to have difficulties with falls, particularly falling backward. The disease also tends to progress much faster than typical Parkinson's disease. People with PSP typically develop difficulty with the movement of their eyes and may have problems aiming their eyes at the object or person they're trying to focus on. They also tend to have a distinct difficulty with *vertical* movement of their eyes, meaning they become unable to voluntarily shift their gaze up or down. Additionally, they can experience blurred vision or double vision as a result of motor difficulties involving the muscles around the eyes. This combined with the balance problems that are present in the disorder can lead to a serious risk for falls. Aside from falls, people with PSP may have a hard time eating their food without spilling, or accomplishing tasks that require a lot of hand-eye coordination. Problems with rigidity in the voluntary facial muscles can also cause individuals with PSP to acquire a permanent facial expression that looks like shock or surprise. Unfortunately, since slurred speech is another common symptom of PSP, individuals who experience it are sometimes mistaken for being drunk due to the combination of speech and balance issues.

Cognitive issues and dementia are also sometimes present in PSP. These issues often look similar to those seen in frontotemporal degeneration, but are usually more mild. People with PSP-driven dementia often have disinhibition, in which they are not able to hold back impulsive tendencies, and they will also have trouble with organization and planning. Another similarity to frontotemporal degeneration is that they may display inappropriate emotions, known as pseudobulbar affect, in which they laugh or cry for no apparent reason. In general, their emotional responses might be exaggerated and disproportionate to the situation. So they may cry hysterically at a somewhat sad commercial or have an extreme laughing fit at something only mildly humorous.

In general, progressive supranuclear palsy begins earlier than many other disorders. The age of onset for PSP is often 40 years or younger. This is another progressive disorder, and people are expected to survive about 7 years after its onset. However, as mentioned, the onset can be notoriously difficult to pinpoint due to the unique nature of PSP. Therefore, to families it can sometimes seem like the disorder comes out of nowhere and progresses very rapidly when it truly started several years earlier and went undetected. Medication is not very helpful for PSP. The medications that are used to help with motor difficulties in Parkinson's disease can be applied here, but they only help for about 2 to 3 years and can be less effective overall than they would be for someone with regular Parkinson's.

Huntington's Disease

Dementia can also come from inherited genetic disorders such as Huntington's disease. If you have a parent with Huntington's, there is a 50 percent chance you will develop it. The primary issue with Huntington's is that it ultimately kills the neurons in your brain. This process begins in an area of your brain called the basal ganglia, which is responsible mainly for managing movement and behavioral control, issues with emotions, personality, and motor skills are the first things affected. Generally, the first symptoms for someone with Huntington's are mood difficulties such as irritability, mood swings, anger, and depression. From there, they will begin to have difficulties with memory. As the disease progresses, the thinking difficulties expand from simple forgetfulness and the person will develop problems with their judgment and decision making. Later in the disease process, the types of thinking difficulties are harder to tease apart, since the entire brain begins to break down and nearly every function becomes impaired.

Movement issues are also present in Huntington's disease, but they differ from those seen in Parkinsonian conditions. People with Huntington's may have familiar symptoms such as an unsteady walking pattern and balance difficulties, but they also have a unique type of motor problem called chorea (pronounced like the country Korea). Chorea is the Greek word for "dance," which the disorder sometimes resembles. The movements in chorea are typically jerky, writhing, and less repetitive than those seen in Parkinson's disease. These movements can happen throughout the body including the head, arms, and torso, rather than in one localized area such as the hands. It's somewhat hard to explain the difference on paper, so we suggest you take a look at some of the great videos online. All you have to do is go to youtube.com and search for "Huntington's chorea" and you will find some examples.

Huntington's disease is a difficult disorder. It is considered fatal in that we currently have no cure for it and it eventually deteriorates a person's abilities to the point that they are too weak to sustain life. The disorder also tends to appear frighteningly early, with an onset somewhere between the ages of 30 and 50. The disease then gets progressively worse over about 10 to 25 years. Unfortunately, there are no treatments that can change the course of Huntington's disease. However, there are several medications that can help a person suffering from the disorder to better cope with the movement symptoms and psychiatric symptoms that come along with it. These help improve the person's quality of life, but ultimately the disease will continue to progress under the surface regardless of the medication taken. Similarly, people can undergo physical therapy and other interventions to help them cope with the symptoms of Huntington's. Interventions can help counteract the impact of the disease, but they will not stop the neurons from breaking down in the brain, and all people with the disease will eventually lose the ability to function. A grim prospect to be sure, but that's the reality of the situation at the present moment. For people with a parent who has the disorder, genetic testing is available to determine your risk. However, this typically does not help to change the course of the disease or identify when the onset might occur. Some people find that they would just rather know.

Vascular Dementia

For most of this chapter, we have talked about dementia that comes as the result of some disorder that breaks down the functioning of the brain progressively. Now we want to mention a couple of ways someone can acquire dementia without one of these disorders. More particularly, we will focus on vascular dementia (due to issues with blood vessels) and traumatic brain injury. Let's start with vascular dementia. There are many forms of vascular dementia. Basically, the overarching concept is that any disorder, disease, or damage that affects the blood vessels in your brain can cause impairment in thinking skills, and in some cases, impairment severe enough to cause dementia.

Most of you are probably familiar with the concept of strokes. A stroke is also sometimes referred to as a cerebral vascular accident (CVA) and involves a stoppage in the blood flow to your brain. This can be caused by a blood clot that plugs up a blood vessel in the brain or by a blood vessel that breaks and bleeds into the brain. The common symptoms of a stroke are sudden numbness or weakness, often occurring on one side of the body, confusion, difficulty with communication, vision problems, dizziness and loss of coordination, and extreme headaches. When someone has a stroke, the cells within the brain are at risk of dying due to lack of blood flow. Since a stroke can occur in many different places within the brain, the type of impairment you see afterward is dependent on where that stroke happened. Early intervention at a hospital is vital when someone has a major stroke because the doctors will work to break up clots, stop bleeding, and restore blood flow to the brain with the hopes of minimizing permanent damage. For many people, rehabilitation after a stroke can help restore much of their functioning, but for some who have severe strokes, repeated strokes, or do not get appropriate medical care, they can experience permanent thinking difficulties that rise to the level that would be considered dementia.

Dementia caused by a stroke can look similar to all of the different dementia types we have gone through so far in this chapter, if the stroke occurred in the same part of the brain affected by the similar dementia condition. For instance, if the stroke was in the temporal lobe, a person might have difficulties with language and memory that can be reminiscent of Alzheimer's disease. Fortunately, unlike Alzheimer's disease (or many of the other diseases we have mentioned), strokes and cerebrovascular disease are not considered progressive conditions. While they can worsen over time, they don't inevitably break down the brain. Instead, the prognosis depends on the person's general cardiovascular health. The body is one single unit, including the brain.

More subtle vascular issues can also cause thinking difficulties. You have probably heard the terms "gray matter" and "white matter." Gray matter refers to the tissue of the brain mostly on the cortex (outside) that contains the main body of the neurons. White matter refers to tissue in that subcortical (inside) space that we talked about previously and it mostly contains the axons (long part of the neuron) that connect the different parts of the brain together. Fun fact: the reason white matter is white is that these axons are covered in a fatty material that helps the nerve impulses travel more quickly. As we mentioned in the chapter on normal aging, the interconnections between parts of the brain begin to break down as we get older. This is formally referred to as "white matter disease." Some white matter disease is expected with normal aging and would not be expected to cause major problems. However, cardiovascular issues and genetic risk factors can create more white matter disease than is typical for a given age. In cases with extensive white matter disease, you can get cognitive impairment that looks a lot like the subcortical dementias, such as Parkinson's dementia. That is, the efficiency of the person's thinking skills can decrease, and they might experience trouble with thinking speed, attention, learning new information, and even motor or balance issues. White matter disease can get worse if cardiovascular issues are not well controlled. Due to the aging process, we would expect white matter disease to progress to some extent, but taking good care of your blood pressure, blood sugar, and other cardiovascular factors can help slow that progression.

Vascular dementia is very common. The estimates and prevalence rates are constantly shifting, but it is likely the second or third most common type of dementia. The effects vary due to the fact it can affect both the cortical and subcortical regions. Vascular dementia can also coexist with other types of dementia such as that seen in Alzheimer's disease. When that happens, we call it a "mixed dementia." There are many different types of mixed dementia, but vascular with Alzheimer's is the most common. In this type of mixed dementia, you would see greater impairment in thinking skills and a faster decline than you would normally expect to see with one disorder alone. Luckily, there are some obvious risk factors that can be addressed to prevent the likelihood of developing vascular dementia. If your loved one has high blood pressure, diabetes, or high cholesterol, it may be worth pursuing medical treatment, regardless of whether they are starting to show signs of cognitive impairment.

Brain Injury

Finally, we would like to briefly mention brain injuries. A traumatic brain injury occurs when you have disruption of normal functioning due to some sort of trauma to the brain. There are many different types of brain injuries; some more severe than others. A brain injury could be caused by a bump or blow directly to the head, by something penetrating the skull (like a bullet or metal rod), or by the brain jostling violently within the skull as can be seen in whiplash injuries. The effects of a traumatic brain injury vary widely depending on which area of the brain is affected and how severe the damage is. In some cases, there's a general decrease in thinking efficiency and speed of processing that does not cause significant disruption. In others, you can see full blown dementia. Just like with vascular dementia, dementia caused by a traumatic brain injury can mimic the other dementias mentioned in this chapter. For instance, we have seen individuals with injuries to their frontal lobes who end up demonstrating the same sort of impairment seen in frontotemporal degeneration, such as behavioral problems, difficulty with mental organization, and personality changes. It's common to see people with frontal brain injuries start to act in inappropriate ways that do not fit with the person they were before their accident. We have also seen people in our practice who have language impairment reminiscent of that seen in Alzheimer's disease due to an injury to the temporal lobes.

The human brain is amazing and has the capacity to heal from many types of traumatic brain injury. Typically, the recovery process is fast and significant for the first six months and slows down a bit from there. People will usually reach their full recovery within one to two years. They may or may not recover all their previous abilities, but after two years, their level of recovery will tend to plateau. Since we are talking about an isolated injury, thinking skills should not continue to worsen provided no further damage occurs. That said, having a brain injury could interact with other types of dementia and worsen the overall outcome, similar to mixed vascular dementias. Brain injuries can also have an additive effect, in which they get worse as you continue to have repeated injuries. We see this in the NFL and with professional fighters who have frequent concussions. If you repeatedly expose the brain to trauma without letting it heal, the risk of thinking issues seems to increase exponentially. In some cases, moderate or severe traumatic brain injuries seem to make the brain less resilient, and increase the risk of developing Alzheimer's disease. If you must exposure your brain to trauma, keep the damage mild and give your brain a chance to heal before you hurt it again.

Well, you made it. That was a long, information-heavy chapter. You don't need to memorize this information, but you should come back to this chapter and use it as a reference if you need to. By now you should also have a good feel for the difference between cortical vs subcortical and progressive vs non-progressive dementias. There are other types of dementia that we did not cover here, but these are some of the major players. We must emphasize that you should use the information contained in this chapter as a loose guide and as a jumping off point. You should not use this information as a basis for diagnosis. Leave that to the professionals. The descriptions in this chapter instead serve as valuable background information that will better allow you to identify the warning signs of dementia conditions and help you to understand what a doctor might describe to you (they aren't always the best at explaining these terms clearly). We will talk more about the process of diagnosis and how you can best interact with the professionals involved in later chapters, but for now let's discuss some other non-dementia conditions that can mimic the symptoms of dementia.

6

Conditions That Can
Look Like Dementia

One of the most important parts of the process when you are trying to identify whether someone has developed a dementia condition is ruling out other factors that could be causing the impairment. We have some good and bad news for you. The bad news is, there are several conditions and disorders that can masquerade as dementia and make diagnosis more complicated. The good news is that the majority of these conditions are temporary, and the impairment in thinking skills stops once the disorder is treated. Typically, it is a medical difficulty that will cause this sort of impairment. This can trip people up because they jump to the conclusion of dementia due to the symptoms of memory loss, confusion, or disorientation.

It's best to start from the bottom in the diagnosis process. Have you heard of Occam's razor? It's a problem-solving principle that says when you have two competing guesses, it is typically the one with the fewest assumptions that should be selected. In other words: What's the simple answer? Rather than making the logical leap all the way to a dementia condition, first consider the "simple explanation" that there is a medical problem that could explain all the symptoms you are seeing. In this chapter we will explore some of these potentially confusing conditions. We will not cover all the disorders that could possibly cause cognitive impairment, but we will do our best to cover some of the most common ones you are likely to encounter in a loved one.

Delirium

Many of the medical conditions that we will discuss result in *delirium*. Delirium is a temporary state of seriously diminished mental abilities that is caused by some physical issue. Usually delirium will come on suddenly, as opposed to the sneaky and gradual onset of something like Alzheimer's disease. The duration is variable. Some medical issues will cause a very brief and severe period of delirium that lasts for just hours. Others have effects that persist over a week or more. A good example of short-term delirium would be what you see with fevers. Perhaps you have seen this in yourself or a family member. When you have a fever that gets too high, you may experience confusion, disorientation, and even hallucinations. That's where the term "fever dream" comes from. I (Dr. Duff) can remember one severe fever I had in college that progressed to a temporary state of delirium. It probably was not the best idea to lie in bed and watch *A Clockwork Orange* for the first time during that illness! I awoke completely disoriented and terrified by the blurred line between the disturbing dreams caused by the movie and the present reality.

On the other hand, many different types of infections are responsible for longer lasting periods of delirium. In clinical practice, one of the most common scenarios we see is elderly people with urinary tract infections (UTIs). For multiple reasons, as we reach old age, our bodies have a particularly difficult time handling UTIs and we can develop symptoms that look very much like dementia, including disruption in memory, agitation, and general confusion. We have had situations where we were called in to assess someone who suddenly developed symptoms that seemed very much like severe dementia, only to come back a few weeks later to see the person back to their normal self after being treated for an infection. While UTIs are treatable, aging bodies have a harder time bouncing back from them, and recurrent UTIs can increase the rate of progression in elders who are already developing a dementia condition. If your loved one has a compromised immune system or chronic health conditions, stay on top of their medical care to reduce their risk of developing the shocking symptoms of delirium.

Case Study – Delirium:
Josie is a 67-year-old woman who lives on her own near family members. She functions normally for her age and enjoys playing bridge, seeing movies, and frequent dinners with friends. One night around 10 p.m., Josie called her daughter frantic and scared. She wasn't able to articulate what was wrong, but told her daughter to come over quickly.

When Josie's daughter arrived, she found Josie on the couch looking around frantically. Josie wouldn't make normal eye contact, was clearly agitated, and kept begging to go home (she was already in her home of many years). Eventually, Josie admitted she felt like the walls and shadows were closing in, causing a sense of unbearable dread.

Josie's daughter called the paramedics to investigate what was causing her mother's frightening state. When the paramedics arrived, they asked some simple questions that revealed Josie was extremely confused. She couldn't recall her daughter's name and became hysterical when asked where she was, again begging to be taken home. Josie was taken to the hospital where she received a full medical evaluation.

It was revealed she had a severe urinary tract infection that was causing a temporary state of delirium. She was discharged after two days in the hospital. Josie's daughter stayed with her for a few days, after which she seemed to make a full recovery and no longer expressed the same fears and concerns.

Metabolic problems can also contribute to changes in thinking skills. To clarify, the term *metabolic* refers to the combination of all the chemical reactions that occur in our bodies to keep our systems working. It's a broad category, but there are a couple of metabolic issues in particular that frequently cause issues resembling dementia.

Thyroid

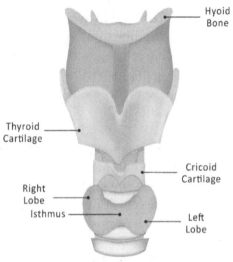

One of the most important glands in the body is called the thyroid. It's a structure in your neck that secretes hormones that influence many different systems in the body and plays a role in your body's overall metabolic rate. When there is too little thyroid hormone, we call it hypothyroidism (literally meaning under-thyroid). Hypothyroidism can cause a host of symptoms reminiscent of depression including fatigue, muscle weakness, irritability, weight gain, slowed speed of thinking, and memory loss. Severe hypothyroidism can even mimic dementia. In general, hypothyroidism is treated with relative ease through medication. Hypothyroidism can be the result of several different factors, but one of the most common is an autoimmune disorder called Hashimoto's disease in which your body's own antibodies attack the thyroid gland. In general, once the thyroid hormones are brought back to an acceptable level via medication, the thinking changes that may have arisen due to hypothyroidism will ease up. If you have questions about thyroid functioning in you or your loved one, please talk with your doctor about having tests run. Our explanation here is a very basic one and there are many factors to consider in the treatment of thyroid dysfunction.

Another metabolic disease we should mention is Wilson's disease. This is an interesting genetic disorder that causes too much copper to accumulate in your body. Symptoms are usually related to an accumulation of copper in the liver and brain. The liver symptoms include physical issues such as vomiting, weakness, yellowing of the skin, itchiness, and swelling. From the brain, we can see a variety of symptoms including tremors, muscle stiffness, personality changes, anxiety, hallucinations, and communication problems.

Since this is a genetic disorder, inherited from an affected gene in both parents, diagnosis typically relies on an accurate family history. In the absence of a clear family history of the disease, diagnosis can be tricky since the symptoms that we mentioned could represent a wide variety of conditions such as Parkinson's disease, hypothyroidism, Alzheimer's disease, or Lewy body disease. This disease is treatable through dietary changes as well as chelation treatment. Basically, chelation involves a medication that binds to copper and causes you to expel it through urine. When appropriately treated, the cognitive symptoms of Wilson's disease would not get worse over time. However, left untreated or inaccurately diagnosed, a person's thinking skills and behaviors could continue to deteriorate. In certain situations, liver transplants are used to cure the disease. Transplants are typically not pursued in cases involving severe brain-related symptoms, as there seems to be little benefit to the individual.

Nutritional Deficiencies

Nutritional deficiencies can also lead to symptoms similar to dementia conditions. By nutritional deficiencies, we mean certain vitamins that are not adequately supplied by the person's diet, or that the person is unable to appropriately absorb from the food they eat. One of the most commonly deficient vitamins is B12, also known as cobalamin. B12 is important for the formation of red blood cells in your body as well as the normal functioning of the brain and nervous system. As we age, our ability to absorb B12 from food can weaken, so this is a nutritional factor that is always important to consider in an elder who seems to be declining. People who have had gastric surgeries (surgeries of the stomach) may also be at risk for developing vitamin B12 deficiency. Of course, this can also be caused by simply not consuming enough of the vitamin, which may happen in certain vegan diets or in people who are generally malnourished. The effects of B12 deficiency are wide ranging and can include muscle weakness, decreased memory, depression, and irritability. Fortunately, this condition is relatively easy to treat with supplementation, either in pill form or through injection, and cognitive symptoms typically improve when there is no longer a deficiency of the vitamin.

Vitamin B1, otherwise known as thiamine, is also linked to cognitive changes. Our bodies only store small amounts of B1, so it depletes relatively quickly. The consequences of thiamine deficiency can be quite severe, leading to coma and even death in some cases. You can become deficient in thiamine due to malnutrition, high intake of foods that break down thiamine, such as raw shellfish and freshwater fish, or through chronic alcoholism.

Let's talk about alcohol abuse and thiamine for a moment. The cells in your nervous system require thiamine, and chronic overuse of alcohol can reduce the body's ability to transport, store, and break down thiamine. This can lead to a variety of neurological disorders, the most common of which is called Wernicke-Korsakoff syndrome (WKS). This is the name for two disorders that often occur together and it's one that we have seen numerous times in our clinical practice. WKS is often seen in alcoholics who go on a bender and combine heavy drinking with poor nutrition for multiple days. In WKS you will often see serious vision impairment due to weakness or paralysis of the muscles responsible for eye movement. People with WKS also demonstrate problems with their gait and stance, symptoms collectively referred to as ataxia. They frequently experience confusion, amnesia, language difficulties (aphasia), trouble recognizing the meaning of objects (agnosia), and difficulty performing previously simple movements such as brushing one's teeth (apraxia).

Regarding memory impairment, with WKS you most often see anterograde amnesia, which means difficulty creating new memories after the illness occurred ("antero" means after). In some cases, especially when not treated quickly enough, you also see retrograde amnesia, which means difficulty recalling events and memories from prior to the illness. For example, someone with retrograde amnesia might forget where they work or where they have lived for the past 5 years. This sometimes creates a difficult situation where patients in our clinical practice are unable to access memories of their chronic alcohol abuse due to the fact that they have retrograde amnesia. In these cases, the person has difficulty believing they ever had an alcohol problem or were hospitalized, and can be very confused about why people are making such a big deal.

Wernicke-Korsakoff's Syndrome
- A potentially severe brain disorder caused by lack of thiamine/vitamin B1.
- Frequently caused by malnutrition or chronic alcoholism.
- Causes numerous symptoms including:
  - Visual impairment.
  - Ataxia (trouble walking and with stance while standing).
  - Cognitive issues such as amnesia, confusion, language difficulties, and trouble performing actions.
  - Treatable when thiamine is administered early enough.

Wernicke-Korsakoff's syndrome is a potentially severe disorder, and its onset is considered a treatment emergency. When someone is experiencing Wernicke's encephalopathy (which describes half of the disorder we just mentioned), they need to receive thiamine supplementation immediately. In general, thiamine treatment can reduce the progression of difficulties, but it won't reverse the issues that have already developed. Thiamine can be administered by mouth or through an injection. While it may not resolve memory loss that has already set in, it can significantly decrease the intense confusion or delirium that can happen with WKS.

Without proper treatment, WKS continues to steadily progress to the point of becoming life threatening. If you have any indication that your loved one may be experiencing symptoms similar to what we described here, take them to a medical provider to be tested for the disorder as soon as possible.

Normal Pressure Hydrocephalus

Just like nearly every other technical name for problems with the brain, this one sounds scary. Normal pressure hydrocephalus (NPH) is a brain disorder in which excess fluid accumulates in the brain. Your brain has little pockets of space inside it called ventricles. In a normally functioning person, there is a fluid called cerebrospinal fluid (CSF) that acts as a cushion and buffer for the brain. It is generated within these hollow ventricles and circulates throughout the brain and spinal cord. In addition to serving as a shock absorber, CSF serves other important functions, such as providing immune support for the brain. The term hydrocephalus translates to "water brain," which pretty clearly describes the issue. There are a variety of hydrocephalus conditions, but in normal pressure hydrocephalus, the pressure of the fluid in the body stays normal. Instead of increasing pressure in the skull, the excess fluid causes those ventricles in the brain to swell, changing the shape of the brain. As the ventricles increase in size, they essentially push against the surrounding parts of the brain, squeezing them against the inside of the skull.

There are three hallmark symptoms of normal pressure hydrocephalus: walking difficulty, changes in thinking skills, and loss of bladder control (also called urinary incontinence). The style of walking often seen in NPH is sometimes described as if the person were walking on a boat, with a wide stance, shuffling steps, and forward-bent body. Thinking changes typically include overall slowing of cognitive abilities, impaired planning and decision making, concentration issues, and emotional symptoms such as apathy.

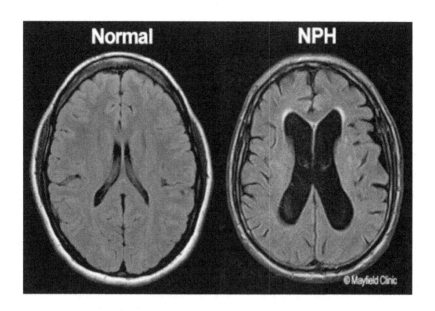

In order to diagnose NPH, doctors look for these cardinal symptoms as well as evidence of swollen ventricles on brain imaging. Treatment involves the use of a shunt, which is a tube that allows the excess fluid to drain from the brain down into the abdomen. Typically, once the shunt is placed, ventricles get smaller in a matter of days. Despite the reduction of swelling and excess fluid, the extent to which a person with NPH can reduce their symptoms varies quite a bit. Some people experience marked improvement and some may only see partial improvement in one specific symptom. While NPH can happen to people of any age, it's most often seen in the elderly population and typically occurs around age 60 or 70.

Adverse Medication Side Effects

In the field of psychiatry we say there is no such thing as a biochemical free lunch. In non-nerd talk, that means a medication that has a particular intended effect is likely to cause side effects. This is because we are not yet able to perfectly increase or decrease chemicals in one particular part of the brain without also creating that effect in other areas of the brain. Some medication side effects are relatively mild, such as headaches or upset stomach. In other cases, the side effects can be more intrusive. There is one class of side effects called anticholinergic effects. Acetylcholine is the main chemical messenger (neurotransmitter) your body uses for muscle activation. In the brain, it's also involved in memory formation. The term anticholinergic means something blocks the functioning of acetylcholine in the body, which can have some pretty rough side effects including confusion and impaired short-term memory, as well as drowsiness and dry mouth. Common drugs that have anticholinergic effects include antihistamines, some older types of antidepressants called tricyclics, and even some medications for Parkinson's disease.

Regardless of age, benzodiazepines are another class of medications that can cause significant side effects. These medications are commonly prescribed for difficulties with anxiety or sleep. Benzodiazepines can be effective for these problems when used appropriately, which means for a short period of time to get someone through a rough patch. Unfortunately, many people use them habitually, and even for any general type of discomfort. The more someone uses these medications, the more likely they will begin to experience their side effects, especially as they develop a tolerance and begin to use them more frequently or at a higher dosage. Benzodiazepines work by inhibiting (calming) the nervous system. This is what you want when someone is having a panic attack. However, they calm the whole nervous system, which can result in adverse effects including sedation, balance and coordination difficulties, slurred speech and vision problems, difficulty with learning and processing information, and general confusion. You can probably see how these lead to bigger problems, like a greater tendency to fall or the appearance of being cognitively impaired.

If you turn on the news these days, it won't be long before you hear something about the opioid crisis. Opioid pain medications were thought initially to be a great advance in the control of chronic pain that would be less addictive than other medications, but that was quickly proven wrong. They are addictive and, without appropriate care in prescribing and intervention, can steal away people's' lives. Besides the issues with addiction, these medications can have a significant effect on thinking skills even when used appropriately. Depending on the dose used, difficulties can range from sedation, to physical slowing, to outright confusion or delirium. And of course, as we use these medications consistently over time, the body builds up a tolerance for them, necessitating higher doses and making these adverse effects more likely to occur. This is NOT a disclaimer to avoid use of opiate medication. Sometimes they are necessary. If your loved one must be on one of these medications, it is vital they follow their doctor's instructions closely and work to remain on the medication for as short a time as possible.

Pseudodementia and Emotional Issues

Most people realize that someone who is experiencing emotional difficulties such as depression or anxiety can seem a bit out of it. However, in our experience, many people are surprised to find out that emotional issues can impact thinking to the extent that it seems as though the person has a dementia condition. When things reach this level, we call it "pseudodementia," which basically means there is a condition masquerading as dementia. With cognitive changes due to depression, the person tends to have a greater awareness of the problems they're experiencing than they would in "true" dementias. As we mentioned in the section on Alzheimer's disease, some forms of dementia lead people to be completely unaware of their difficulties, as if they were in denial (lack of insight). In depressive pseudodementia, the person can be over-sensitive to changes they think they see. Often people in this situation will be more concerned about "losing it" than their families are. Another difference is that many forms of dementia creep in over time and gradually get worse, whereas the onset of depressive pseudodementia is typically abrupt. It can sometimes be associated with a major stress, such as the loss of a spouse or a change in independence, but it doesn't have to be. One positive aspect of pseudodementia is that when the depression is treated or resolves, the person's memory and thinking skills generally return to normal. The following table will demonstrate some ways in which pseudodementia can differ from a true dementia.

	Dementia	Depression
Onset	Subtle/Gradual	Clearly Known
Symptom Progression	Slow	Fast
Complaints	Unusual	Frequent
Awareness	Diminished	Intact
Night Confusion	Common	Variable
Location Disorientation	Common	Unusual
Time Disorientation	Persistent	Fluctuating
Loss of Libido	Variable	Common/Significant
Difficulty Dressing	Common	Unusual

This marks the end of our discussion about non-dementia conditions that can look a lot like dementia. The moral of the story here is that it is absolutely worth digging deeper and doing your due diligence when you have a loved one who seems to be developing cognitive difficulties. If there is a simple solution to the problems, such as a medication change or vitamin supplementation, wouldn't you want to know? It can seem a little scary that there are so many situations that can cause someone impairment, but remember that most of the scenarios we discussed in this chapter are relatively simple to diagnose, as long as your loved one's medical providers are kept in the loop and have the information they need.

Speaking of medical providers, in the next chapter, we are going to discuss the process of working with doctors to get your loved one an accurate diagnosis.

7

Working with Doctors
for a Diagnosis

Recognizing the signs of dementia is one thing, but we find that many family members have no idea what to do when they notice a loved one seems to be suffering from impairment. It's easy to overlook the first signs of decline and attribute them to stress or normal aging. Eventually though, these difficulties become noticeable enough that you may want your parent or loved one to be evaluated. Unfortunately, we frequently find that our patients and family members put off evaluation because they don't know how to get help or what to expect. It can absolutely be overwhelming and it's typically something that you don't know how to navigate unless you've been through it before. In this chapter we will alleviate some of that confusion and hopefully reduce any fear you might have by laying out the normal course of care when you first approach a doctor about memory problems. We will explore how to get started, what specialists you might see, and what types of tests may be conducted. We will look into how a diagnosis usually comes about and some of the common treatment recommendations. Finally, and most importantly, we will provide some strategies for how you can communicate with the doctor. If you haven't noticed, some doctors can be...unique, or at least very busy. We will provide you with some real-world suggestions on how to talk to your loved one's doctor so they don't annoy you and you don't annoy them.

The Initial Workup

When in doubt, start with primary care. Once your loved one is ready to meet with someone about their condition, accompany them to an appointment with their primary care doctor. We often find that elders have the best relationship with their primary care doctor and may feel most comfortable sharing their concerns with someone that they have worked with for a long time. This is especially important when the person is distrustful of being evaluated or meeting with unfamiliar doctors. Primary care is a great way to get the ball rolling.

The doctor will usually start with a basic medical exam. They will review the person's medical history and current symptoms. This is one of the reasons to have someone accompany them to the appointment when possible. As we mentioned earlier, when a person has dementia they may have limited awareness of their symptoms. Having a family member there to give another view on the situation can be crucial. Mention any changes in cognitive, emotional, or physical functioning, as this may give the doctor vital insight into your loved one's condition. The doctor will also want to know about any family history of dementia or conditions that affect thinking skills. Your loved one will likely be asked about their current substance use (even if mild) and medications. Make sure to share everything that they take, including supplements and alternative remedies (like herbs or oils). We have seen patients not mention these, as they feel no need to talk about over-the-counter substances, only to find out later that a supplement was interacting with one of their medications. During this history-gathering process, keep in mind that the doctor will likely ask a series of questions, but at any point you can also bring up any issues you have observed and are concerned about. Better to tell the doctor, rather than leave something out that might affect their diagnosis. We have encountered many situations in our practice where it is clear that someone does not want to speak up due to fear of upsetting their loved one. If this is the case, find some way to get that information to the doctor, even if that means leaving a note for them or pulling them aside in the hallway before you leave.

After collecting a thorough medical history, the doctor will usually progress to a physical and neurological examination. This may include things you are familiar with, such as checking your loved one's blood pressure or breathing, but they will also usually look at nervous system functioning by checking things such as balance and physical sensation. The doctor will also order some basic tests, such as a blood test to check hormone and vitamin levels. Remember, some deficiencies, like vitamin B-12, can significantly affect memory. If you have concerns that the doctor may not be taking the situation seriously or seems to not be thorough, feel free to ask them whether they are planning on running additional tests. Some doctors will take a shotgun approach where they do a thorough examination and run tests right away. Others will move one step at a time so that they don't make the patient feel like they are being put through the wringer.

Additionally, the doctor will usually complete a brief screening measure of mental status. This is a 10–15-minute test involving evaluation of basic concentration skills, language skills, and memory. It can help identify obvious problems or concerns to help the doctor determine if a more thorough evaluation, like a neuropsychological assessment, is required. Common cognitive screening measures you might encounter include the Mini Mental State Exam (MMSE) and the Montreal Cognitive Assessment (MOCA). The doctor may also order some basic brain imaging, such as a brain MRI or CT scan, to look for obvious signs of damage to the brain, such as from a stroke. We see some families try to coach their loved one on how to succeed at these tests. We would advise against this. For significantly impaired individuals the coaching may not help, but for those in the mild cognitive impairment range, you may be helping your loved one hide their impairment from the doctor.

102

These are all basic screening measures to start the process of figuring out what is going on. Based on this initial evaluation, the doctor will probably have some guesses about the main issues. If they have concerns at this point, they will either order some more specific tests or, depending on the doctor's experience with dementia, refer you to a specialist like a neurologist or geriatrician. We know that all of the terminology and different types of doctors can be a bit confusing. Even people within the medical field sometimes use these terms incorrectly. Here is a quick and simple guide to the most common care providers you will interact with on this journey toward a diagnosis.

Procedure	Goals and Tips
Review medical history and current symptoms	Make sure a knowledgeable family member attends.
Neurological exam	Examines sensory and motor skills to detect nervous system problems.
Mini Mental State Assessment	A brief screening test of memory and cognitive skills that usually takes 10–15 minutes.
Blood work	Looks for nutritional deficiencies, metabolic problems, and infections (think delirium).
Brain imaging	A CT or MRI looking for obvious issues like a stroke or other damage.
Referral to other providers	If needed, your doctor will refer you to a neurologist or other specialists.

Dementia Doctors

We all have, or should have, a primary care doctor. This is the physician for most of our medical care, who hopefully gets to know you over time. Primary care doctors often are generalists (competent in many different aspects of medicine), who may have a specialty in internal medicine or family practice. As they age, some people develop conditions that require frequent care or monitoring and may choose a specialist as their primary doctor. This might include a cardiologist for someone with heart issues or an oncologist for someone with cancer. For many seniors it is a good idea to have a primary care doctor who is a specialist in geriatrics, known as a geriatrician. This type of specialist understands how the body changes later in life and is well equipped to manage care for an elderly person. For example, as we age, our metabolism changes, which can affect how we respond to medication. A geriatrician should be sensitive to these nuances.

When it comes to specialists, the most common referral your loved one will receive is to a neurologist, who specializes in disorders of the brain and the overall nervous system. Neurologists often take over and manage the process of diagnosing and treating dementia once an initial evaluation has been done by a primary care doctor. They can't do everything by themselves though, and may refer patients to specialists who'll perform various types of assessments to help fill in the diagnostic picture. These specialists then report back to the neurologist, who gathers the information to make the overall diagnosis and treatment recommendations. The process of diagnosing dementia requires consideration of several different sources of information. You might think of it like a wheel, with the neurologist in the middle and spokes going out to different specialists.

The most common step after seeing a neurologist is to be sent for some brain imaging (radiology). Sometimes this step is taken care of by the primary care doctor, but even if that is the case, your loved one's neurologist may want to do more extensive imaging to look at specific aspects of the brain. We will talk a bit more about these scans later, but first let's acknowledge the radiologists. Radiologists are the medical specialists who interpret the images of the brain in comparison to what would be considered a healthy brain, and sometimes in comparison to previous images of your loved one's brain. Interestingly, you will rarely meet the radiologist in person. The brain imaging is ordered by the neurologist and conducted by a technician, but the radiologist is not usually present. Instead they review the scans that have been completed and provide a written report highlighting what they see as the most significant concerns or interesting features.

Care Provider	Degree Type	Specialty
Primary Care	Physician (MD or DO)	Internal or family medicine practice
Neurologist	Physician (MD or DO)	Brain and its diseases
Neuropsychologist	Psychologist (PhD or PsyD)	Brain's relation to behavior and thinking
Psychiatrist	Physician (MD or DO)	Emotional issues via medication
Psychologist	PhD or PsyD	Emotional issues via therapy
Geriatrician	Physician (MD or DO)	Aging body and associated conditions
Radiologist	Physician (MD or DO)	Using imaging to understand brain structure and function

Brain imaging focuses primarily on the structure of the brain or perhaps overall functioning by looking at brain waves (an EEG) or metabolism (a PET scan). Neither of these tell you much about how a person's brain is actually working though, and that is where we (Dr. Lande and Dr. Duff) come in. We are neuropsychologists, and our job is to examine your thinking skills (such as attention and concentration, memory, and language skills), as well as your mood and behavior, to determine if you are functioning normally for your age. Based on assessment results, we can identify patterns that are common for specific disorders, which can provide crucial information for the diagnosis.

All the other doctors we have mentioned have MDs or DO degrees. MD quite literally means Doctor of Medicine. Pretty straightforward. There is also another medical degree, DO, which means Doctor of Osteopathic Medicine. Both MDs and DOs can practice medicine, perform surgery, and prescribe medications with relatively little significant distinction between them. Now in comparison, neuropsychologists are psychologists who have attained further education in the brain and how it relates to our thinking and behavior. As psychologists, our degrees are either Doctorates in Philosophy (PhD) or in Psychology (PsyD). We are doctors who can diagnosis and treat conditions related to mental health, but we do not prescribe medication. In regard to the dementia evaluation process, we help establish the diagnosis, describe a person's cognitive and emotional strengths and weaknesses, and suggest care and treatment. Following a neuropsychological evaluation, you will typically have a feedback session, which allows us the chance to sit with you and fully discuss the results of the assessment, provide advice, and answer questions.

One last type of specialist your parent might be referred to is the psychiatrist. This is a type of medical doctor, sometimes confused with psychologists, as we both assess and treat mental disorders. A major difference is that psychiatrists can prescribe psychiatric medication, whereas psychologists focus more on psychotherapy and counseling. This is not a perfect distinction, as many psychiatrists also provide psychotherapy and some psychologists can prescribe depending on their state laws. Often your loved one will be referred for psychiatric care if there are significant mood difficulties or behavioral problems either associated with or separate from their dementia. The common line of thinking is that therapy and medication together are more effective than medication alone. However, in aging populations with memory problems or other behavioral issues, sometimes medication needs to be the primary treatment for emotional difficulties, since typical therapy may not fit within their limitations. For example, someone with moderate-severe Alzheimer's disease probably would not benefit from talk therapy because they wouldn't be able to remember what they spoke about during sessions.

Diagnosis

Determining a diagnosis of dementia is generally a process of ruling out conditions. Your loved one's physician will do this by gathering as much information as they can, including exploring leads as they occur. For example, in our practice, we recently saw a woman for assessment of memory loss and concerns about dementia. She reported decreased memory, difficulty focusing, loss of interest in activities, increased isolation, and difficulties managing her affairs. All this started about two years ago, so the first thing we did was try to determine what changed at that point in time. Did these symptoms emerge gradually and sneak up on the family, or did they emerge suddenly in response to a health condition or other stressor? We learned that multiple close family members passed away within a few months of one another. Definitely an important piece of the puzzle.

This sort of history may lead one to suspect depression is causing this person's problems, but it's important to be more thorough. Depression and pseudodementia might be an initial diagnosis, but this will continue to change as more information comes in.

The doctor will look at your loved one's history and those initial medical screeners we discussed to see which potential conditions seem to fit. Once they have the first hypotheses and working diagnoses, they will likely plan a course of assessments to confirm whether the diagnosis is accurate. There is no simple blood test for dementia, or even for the neurological conditions that cause dementia, such as Alzheimer's disease. Instead the physician will need to be thorough in their assessment process by taking pieces of information from the screening measures, medical history, brain imaging, and neuropsychological assessment, and pulling them together to inform a final diagnosis.

Let's take a moment to explore these different assessment tools. The table below offers a brief overview. We'll dive into more detail as the chapter continues.

Assessment	How it Works	What it Tells Us
Computed Tomography Scan (CT)	X-rays are taken of the brain from different angles.	Shows a clear picture of the structure of the brain.
Magnetic Resonance Imaging (MRI)	Magnetic fields are used to get images of the brain from different angles.	Provides pictures of the structure of the brain that have better resolution.
Electroencephalography (EEG)	Electrodes are placed on head to measure electrical discharge.	Records brain activity (waves) to look for seizures and other brain dysfunction.

Positron Emission Tomography (PET) Scan	X-ray scans of the brain monitor tracers to see change over time.	Allows for the study of brain metabolism (activity) in addition to structure.
Neuropsychological Evaluation	Personalized assessment of cognitive skills often using pencil, paper, booklets, etc.	Describes cognitive strengths and weaknesses.

CTs and MRIs

We have already mentioned basic brain imaging, like CT scans and MRIs. Both garnered wide-spread use in the 1980s and both provide images of the brain in slices, though MRIs tend to be better for seeing fine detail. The trade-off is that you might be stuck in an MRI machine for 45 minutes, whereas the CT scan is quick and can even be done at a beside. These two tests also differ in how they work. A CT scan is basically an X-ray. An MRI uses magnetic fields to cause the atoms in your brain to align a certain way. This causes your brain to give off its own magnetic field, which can then be detected and used to create a brain image. CT scans and MRIs are most useful to look at structural damage to the brain, as you might see with a stroke or brain tumor. They can also sometimes show evidence of brain atrophy, as you might see in Alzheimer's disease or frontotemporal degeneration.

Remember that most seniors will show some normal atrophy on scans and that is nothing to worry about. When we see atrophy in specific areas that are associated with a degenerative condition and we are starting to see cognitive changes associated with that condition, we become concerned.

One interesting side note about MRIs: Someone eventually noticed that people seemed to feel better emotionally after having an MRI. This led to the development of transcranial magnetic stimulation, a treatment that uses magnetic fields to stimulate areas of the brain. It is currently used to treat some forms of depression and neuropathic pain.

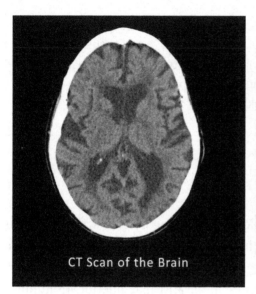
CT Scan of the Brain

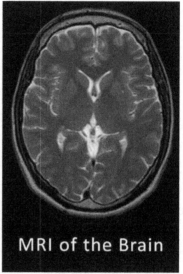
MRI of the Brain

EEG Printout

Another assessment technique during dementia evaluations is electroencephalography (EEG). This test measures your brainwaves, or the bioelectrical activity of your brain via electrodes placed on the scalp. Normal aging does not seem to affect performance on EEG, but conditions that cause cognitive impairment can change EEG results. Even in early cases of dementia or brain dysfunction, slowed rhythm of brain waves can be observed. The information garnered through the EEG tends to be general when it comes to dementia. Rather than helping to identify a specific form, it signals the presence of a general problem. The good thing about it is that it is a quick and painless procedure that many find somewhat relaxing.

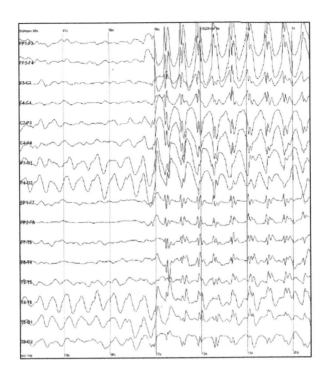

PET Scan

A newer imaging technique that has gained a great deal of prominence is positron emission tomography (PET). CT scans offer a static, or unmoving, snapshot of the brain. PET scans use CT technology, along with injection of a harmless tracer chemical, to develop a video of the brain's functioning, especially in regard to metabolism.

The most common type of PET scan is called fluorodeoxyglucose, or FDG, PET. With this scan, the brain is observed to determine how effectively it is taking up and metabolizing glucose. Glucose is basically the sugar that powers the brain. A PET scan can tell us if certain parts of the brain are not working properly. Depending on the location of this dysfunction, an FDG PET scan can help identify the presence of Alzheimer's disease or frontotemporal degeneration. This does not give us any information about how the person is functioning in their everyday life, but it can help identify the presence of a condition.

111

There is a newer type of PET scan that bears mentioning. Amyloid PET scans function a little differently. In our explanation of Alzheimer's disease, we mentioned amyloid plaques, which are the plaques left behind when neurons in the brain die. The Amyloid PET scan involves a tracer that binds to that amyloid plaque in the brain and shows how much plaque is present. Currently, this type of PET scan is primarily used for clinical research, such as in drug trials, but it is becoming more common as a tool for diagnosis. Notably, Amyloid PET scans can identify the presence of Alzheimer's disease before the person exhibits any clinical impairment. This is a double-edged sword. Finding out that someone may have a serious disease years before they start showing symptoms can cause a great deal of stress and worry. However, it may also provide the opportunity for the person to prepare and engage in the best preventative treatments. As with most imaging techniques, remember that a PET scan is not definitive. It's one piece of the puzzle.

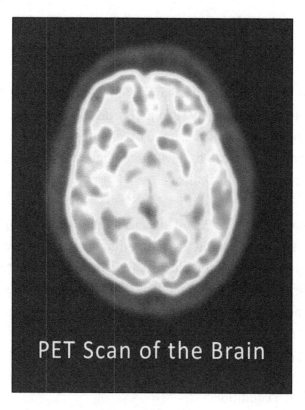

PET Scan of the Brain

The last common type of assessment tool to mention is our specialty, neuropsychological assessment. While imaging focuses on the structure of the brain, neuropsychological assessment focuses on how the brain is working (cognitive ability). Assessments are generally broad and cover areas of functioning such as attention, speed of processing, reasoning skills, language functioning, memory, visuospatial skills, and even emotional functioning.

Neuropsychological Assessment

Unlike the fancy brain scans, neuropsychological assessment is often fairly low tech (though we are seeing an increased in the use of tablets in the assessment process). The time spent on an assessment varies, but you can count on it being somewhat lengthy. In our practice, we are typically spending 3–4 hours with a patient. There are other settings where the assessment process takes even longer. Although it can be tough to sit through such a long process, this really helps us be thorough and understand what is happening for the person. For instance, it may be easy to jump straight to memory as the primary issue, but sometimes problems with attention can be at the root of someone's memory issues, since the information they are getting essentially goes in one ear and out the other without ever being absorbed. The good thing about this type of assessment is that it can be broken up into multiple sessions if the person has a hard time tolerating long appointments or becomes too fatigued to push through. Even during the testing session, it's common to take breaks.

A neuropsychological assessment generally starts with a clinical interview where we discuss a patient's presenting problem and their general medical history. Typically, we like to have a family member or trusted friend with the patient for this portion so we can get multiple sources of information.

It is common for the person being tested to have a different perspective on their situation than a family member or caregiver. When this difference of perspective is contentious or volatile, we can conduct separate interviews so that the person is not highly agitated before starting the tests. We then conduct a series of short tests, most only 5–10 minutes long, that may be verbal, paper and pencil, or involve pointing to items in a booklet. We tend to tailor the tests we choose to the patient depending on their particular situation.

Once the testing is completed, the neuropsychologist will score everything and create a report that documents cognitive strengths and weaknesses, the likely diagnosis, and recommendations for care and treatment. A feedback session is usually provided in which the neuropsychologist will go over the findings and recommendations with you and your parent. While this is the typical structure of a neuropsychological assessment, you will find some variability between providers. Some neuropsychologists will conduct longer assessments. Some will focus less on feedback and more on interfacing directly with the referring doctor. For our practice, we try to make the interview and testing process as short as it can be while still being comprehensive. We also focus on direct feedback with the client so we can explain things in plain language and answer questions that may arise.

Relating to Doctors

We all know that it can sometimes be difficult to communicate with our doctors or understand our healthcare systems. In our experience, several factors go into this, including issues on both the patient and doctor side. For patients and family members, it may be hard to find the motivation to fully participate in the process. It can be terrifying to peel back the layers and figure out whether you have a serious illness, and the process of meeting with countless doctors to get a straight answer can be intimidating. It can feel like torture for some elderly people who, from their perspective, were living a quiet, normal life, when suddenly people started making a big deal about their memory and began forcing them to go to a million boring appointments. It's a natural reaction to be a bit avoidant or stubborn about the process.

On our end as doctors, we sometimes don't make the best effort to sit with someone and clarify the whole situation. It's confusing and even though we see many people with similar issues each week, this is probably the first time you and your loved one have been through this process. There is also an unfortunate tendency among doctors to be a bit intimidating. They may talk over someone, not describe things well, or order tests without fully explaining their reasoning. Doctors are often taught to be "the expert," which can come at the expense of treating patients more like puzzle pieces than fellow humans. There are most certainly some great, personable doctors out there who combine strong clinical skills with wonderful bedside manner, but sometimes it's just luck of the draw. Your options may also be limited depending on how many providers are in your area. In this section we're going to discuss some of the ways you and your loved one can break down barriers and more effectively communicate with your doctors.

This might seem obvious, but the number one thing you can do to aid in this process is accompany your loved one to their appointments. Clearly, the person who is being evaluated must go, but it is important (sometimes essential) that a trusted friend or family member attend as well. There are several reasons for this. As we mentioned, doctor's appointments can be stressful and sometimes rushed. This can make it difficult to remember exactly what was discussed during the appointment or the instructions that the doctor gave you. Therefore, attending appointments with your loved one can help provide a record of what happened during the appointment. A few years ago, I (Dr. Lande) was seeing an orthopedic doctor regarding a shoulder injury. One day I went to an appointment where the doctor was quite behind. It felt like he rushed into the exam room, looked at me for 5 minutes and then sent me on my way. As I got in my car to leave, I realized I had no idea what the doctor's suggestions were for continuing my care. As a normally functioning person, this annoyed me enough to run back into the office and complain, which incidentally lead to an additional 10 minutes of facetime with the doctor and a new MRI order. However, someone with growing issues due to a dementia condition would be more likely to simply move along without ever realizing there was important information they should be taking with them from the appointment. This could lead to significant delays in treatment.

Having a trusted person present with the patient for these types of doctor's appointments can also help treatment since they will be able to give their own opinions about their loved one's recent behaviors or difficulties. As a friend or family member, you may also want to ask questions that the person suffering from possible dementia would not think to ask. While appointments are mainly to help the patient, friends, family, and caregivers can also benefit from the information provided. Often doctors who specialize in these issues have just about seen it all, and can provide helpful information and suggestions to help you learn how to be a better caregiver or support person. In our own practice, we often suggest resources for caregivers and family members before we even finish the testing process.

A good way to stay organized and communicate results to everyone involved is to take a notebook to the appointments. On the first page you can write down answers for demographic questions a physician might have, like date and location of birth, as well as the names of the doctors your loved one is seeing. On the second page it can be useful to record the conditions the patient has, as well as past conditions and surgeries. After that, you can record current medications and dosages. Leave some space between each medication so you can note when they were started, dosage changes, and any concerns you might have about side effects or other issues. Leave space on each page so you can continue to add notes to it over the course of your loved one's care. The rest of the notebook can be used to record medical appointments. You don't need in-depth notes, just reserve a page for each appointment to list any issues that were brought up and any changes in treatment. It is also helpful for caregivers and the patient to write down any questions they might have for the doctor before heading into the appointment. Before the appointment is over, look at the list to make sure all questions were asked and addressed. Using a system like this can be very helpful to track your loved one's care. If different caregivers end up attending appointments, it helps ensure that everyone is recording and communicating information in the same way.

Sometimes caregivers don't feel comfortable speaking in front of their loved one or worry about making them upset. In such cases it's always fine to ask to speak to the doctor separately or prior to the appointment. It's also reasonable to send a note to the doctor expressing concerns you didn't want to say during an appointment, or to let the doctor know about any new issues your loved one might not remember.

Ongoing Care

By the time a final diagnosis is determined, your loved one will probably be pretty tired of seeing doctors. However, it's important to keep up with ongoing care. Obviously, you will want the doctor to monitor the effectiveness of medications and other interventions to know how they are working and if they need to be adjusted. The physician also needs to be able to observe how your loved one's condition is changing over time. Since some forms of dementia are progressive, the patient's needs, and caregivers' needs for support, will change. Often when a patient is stable in their treatment plan the physician will still want to see them every one- to two years to assess if there have been changes that require a new treatment. Some of the initial assessments, such as brain imaging and neuropsychological assessment, may also be repeated multiple times (typically after a year) to see how things are progressing.

In Summary

Hopefully you now see that although the process of getting a diagnosis for memory difficulties or cognitive decline can seem long and frustrating, there is a method to the madness. Your loved one's doctors are trying to be thorough and rule out all possibilities, because dementia conditions are serious and require accurate treatment. In the midst of the confusion and business of achieving an accurate diagnosis, just remember it's all for good reason and worth it to make sure you can move forward with the most appropriate plan.

Finally, before we move on to the next section, we want to acknowledge that, unfortunately, sometimes doctors do not take your concerns seriously. A primary care doctor without a special focus in geriatric care might hear your concerns about your loved one and assume you're being overly sensitive to the normal changes that come along with aging. If your personal research and experience of your loved one in everyday life suggests there is cause for concern, but you simply are not being heard by their doctor, it is completely reasonable to do something about it. In some cases, levelling with the doctor and explaining that you would like to be thorough, even if there is nothing wrong, will get the ball rolling in the right direction. In other situations, a second opinion from another doctor is called for.

8

Current Treatments
and Behavioral Tools

After a working diagnosis has been established, the big question is, "What do we do now?" Unfortunately, there is no cure for Alzheimer's dementia or most other forms of dementia. Once the brain has been damaged by these conditions it is very difficult to recover. However, that does not mean there is no hope. There are a number of experimental studies trying to determine how to prevent or cure Alzheimer's disease along with other types of dementia. As we discussed earlier in this book, some conditions that affect the brain can be reversed or lessened through even simple means, such as improving cerebrovascular health through exercise, diet, and control of blood pressure. For Alzheimer's disease, these improvements in physical health can lessen or slow the effects of the disease, but they will not stop it from getting worse.

Similarly, in the last decade or two several medications have been developed that specifically address some of the brain changes associated with Alzheimer's and other cortical dementias. These medications do not cure the condition, but they can improve an individual's functioning on a day-to-day basis. In addition to these medications, there are several behavioral techniques that can be used to help people with dementia. These techniques can address memory lapses, confusion, or behavioral problems like agitation. Finally, since dementia can affect a loved one's mood, either directly or by causing frustration with their growing limitations, their psychological health must be addressed as well. Let's dive a little deeper into the different treatments for cognitive changes seen in dementia.

Dementia Medications

The current primary medical treatment for cortical dementias such as Alzheimer's is a class of medications called acetylcholinesterase inhibitors. Common types of this medication that you may hear of include Aricept (donepezil), Exelon (rivastigmine), and Razadyne (galantamine). Acetylcholine (ACh) is a chemical messenger in your brain that's essential for learning and memory. When we learn something, neurons rely on ACh to fire their signals. The easiest way to think of it is that ACh signals from one neuron to the next to pass on a message. Again, this is one of the main mechanisms behind how we learn things.

Typically, after a neuron fires, the ACh that is left in the space between neurons (synapse) is broken down by an enzyme called acetylcholinesterase (AChE). The medications we're talking about stop the work of the AChE enzyme. Therefore, there is more ACh floating around in the space between neurons, which makes it easier for neurons to fire again after sending an impulse.

This is a lot of neuro mumbo jumbo, so let's try to make it as simple as possible. Your neurons use a chemical to tell one another to keep sending a message down a certain pathway. Normally, after that chemical does its job, it's eaten back up by a certain enzyme. These medications stop that enzyme from working so that the neurons are ready to fire more quickly. These medications make up for the loss of ACh-producing neurons that can happen in diseases like Alzheimer's. However, as you might guess, they don't repair the neurons that have been lost. Eventually, there simply won't be enough ACh-producing neurons. The AChE-inhibiting medications help your ACh work harder, but if there isn't enough of it in the first place, the effect isn't going to be very noticeable. These medications tend to be effective for several years before tapering off.

> **Dementia Medications: Aricept, Exelon, etc.**
> - Called acetylcholinesterase inhibitors.
> - Acetylcholine (ACh) is a chemical that helps neurons fire.
> - Normally, once ACh helps the neuron fire, it's then broken down by an enzyme.
> - These medications stop that enzyme from breaking down the ACh so there is more of it available to help more neurons fire.
> - This can reduce the impact of memory loss.

One last very important point about the acetylcholinesterase inhibitors. We hear many doctors incorrectly tell people that the medications will slow down the progression of Alzheimer's and other cortical dementias. They do not do this. Current research indicates there is no difference in the overall course of the disease for someone who takes these medications. However, they *can* improve the quality of someone's thinking or behavior for a time. In this way it might seem like the disease is slowing down, but unfortunately, behind the scenes, the progression continues.

Along with the acetylcholinesterase inhibitors, there is another type of medication that works in tandem later in the dementia process. This type of medication is called a glutamate regulator. Glutamate is another neurotransmitter involved in information processing. The main medication in this class is Namenda (memantine). It is often used with the AChE-inhibiting medications after someone has been using them for a while. There are now also medications that combine both of these types, such as Namzaric.

Overall, these medications are meant to maintain and hopefully enhance cognitive functions such as memory and information processing. In addition to the behavioral techniques that we will discuss below, it is possible to improve someone's quality of life with medication, which is important even if there is not yet a cure for the disease they're living with. Now let's look into some of the non-medication strategies that can be helpful.

Active Learning Strategies

Active learning refers to the process of using information in some intentional way in order to better learn or memorize information. Active learning strategies are more effective for people with mild forms of dementia who, with effort, still have the capacity to make new memories. The nice thing about these tools is that they are probably strategies you're familiar with. Most of us use some sort of active memory strategy when studying for exams in school.

One of the best ways to learn and retain new information is to use it right away. A simple active learning strategy is to repeat back what you have just been told. Even better is to paraphrase the information and put it into your own words. This forces your brain to process and manipulate the information, which strengthens the memory pathways. This strategy is simple to use, and you can implement it by asking your loved one to repeat information back. Just make sure you explain the strategy and goals to them and get their agreement first, otherwise they are likely to get a little annoyed with you. Some individuals with dementia start speaking less during conversations, often because it is hard to keep up with everything. In long conversations it can be helpful for the person with dementia to summarize what he or she heard the other person say, and then to confirm it with them. This will both enable the person to better recall what they talked about and prevent misunderstandings. It can also demonstrate that your loved one is listening and cares about what the other person is saying, even if they have some cognitive challenges that make it more difficult.

Writing information down, such as on a calendar, in an address book, or in a journal, is also a good way of practicing the information, especially if someone is having speaking difficulties. It also provides the individual with dementia something to review later if needed. After a conversation, encourage your loved one to write down a few notes about anything of significance in a journal. This process of writing down experiences can serve as an active memory strategy to help them remember, and may also trigger a memory of what was discussed if they review it later on. For example, in our practice, we encounter retired people who have weekly get-togethers with their friends over coffee or a meal. We often encourage them to write down some notes about the conversation immediately afterwards and review last week's notes prior to the next get-together so the topics that were discussed before are at the top of their mind.

To really improve memory retention, your loved one must continue to review and keep practicing the information later. This is the case for anyone trying to improve their memory retention, but it is particularly important for people with memory challenges. When you learn something new, be it a name, a fact, or an upcoming appointment, try to think about it later that day, and also occasionally over the next few days. Reviewing will improve your ability to retain and retrieve this information later.

Organizing information that you want to retain is another way of getting your brain to actively practice and manipulate the information. "Chunking" is a classic mental organization technique that can be used for this purpose. When you are trying to remember a phone number, you usually don't remember all 7 digits individually. Instead, you typically group them into 3- to 4-digit chunks. Chunking can also be used to sort a lot of items into smaller groups based on some commonality. For example, to remember a grocery list, it can be useful to sort the items into categories, such as produce, drinks, protein, and paper products. This makes the list more manageable. When you are at the store, your categorized list triggers your memory. When you recall the category of fruit, your brain may be cued to remember that you needed bananas, apples, and grapes. Similarly, when you remember the category of protein, you might recall that you needed fish and chicken. In this way, your brain only needs to actively hold on to a few categories rather than using brute force to try to remember 12 or more individual items. When you are trying to help your loved one with dementia recall something, try to cue them with the general category rather than giving exact information, and see if that is enough to kick-start their recall. If you can think of a way your loved one could better chunk or mentally organize the information they're having trouble with, share the strategy with them.

General Memory Strategies

Now that we've explored some active learning strategies, let's delve into some ideas for individuals with more significant levels of dementia. Rather than focusing directly on improving memory, people with more significant impairment often respond best to focusing on structure and routine. There is a stereotype that older people become stubborn and set in their ways. To some extent this is true because it's an effective way to work around some of the cognitive changes that happen with normal aging. This rigidness can be even more pronounced in individuals with dementia, who may remain relatively independent, even after becoming cognitively impaired. Typically, this is due to their routines and habits, which are deeply ingrained and help them live a predictable life.

Several times per year, our practice gets calls from family members concerned about their parent's apparent sudden cognitive decline. They will say that they were living independently with no issues and then, BOOM, they suddenly started showing significant signs of dementia. This is unlikely. More commonly, the person has been impaired for quite a while, but the predictability of their life is keeping them going. When the person encounters some sort of change such as traveling out of state with family or the passing of a spouse that they depended on, we see a sudden decline in their level of functioning because their normal routines and habits are not applicable anymore. Depending on the stage of dementia, many people can recover from this abrupt change in functioning after being supported for a few months. They are simply having difficulty adapting to the changes and need help developing new routines that can keep them going.

Use new information right away	Repeat back important information, summarize it and paraphrase it.
Chunk and organize new information	Categorize or group information to make it easier to remember, like a telephone number.
Spaced retrieval	To remember something well, kept thinking about it later, 5 minutes after you learn it, 10 minutes, etc. If you hold it for 15 minutes, you probably have it.

Focusing on helping your loved one establish useful routines can be a great way to support them in their functioning, especially if they've been frustrated by things like losing keys or forgetting where they placed the mail. Here are some strategies that can be helpful:

- Help your loved one create a place for everything and keep everything in its place. Encourage them to always return their belongings to their designated "homes" as soon as your loved one is finished with them. For instance, you might place an unusual looking bowl next to the front door, which is the home for their keys and phone. The strange bowl sticks out from the environment, which can help them to notice it. After some time, the habit of placing their important items in the bowl may stick and become automatic. You could also use small signs such as "new mail" or "pill box" on the wall to draw their attention to the specific location for those items.

- Along with your loved one, create a master list of where things go around the house. Their participation in the process will make it more meaningful for them. After you assign each item a home, write the name of the item and its home on a list. Make sure you organize it, such as alphabetically or by groupings of similar items. Post this master list on a wall or refrigerator so that it's easily found when needed.

- If your loved one frequently struggles with misplacing and losing items in the home, make a point of encouraging them to look at the place where he or she put it and repeat out loud where it was placed several times. Hopefully they can internalize this as a habit in order to better recall where they set things.

To remember tasks, leave notes or reminders in a place your loved one is likely to see them (for example, a sticky note on a mirror or the inside of the front door). Just make sure to remove them when the task is done. Also don't put up so many that they become overwhelming. Many individuals with dementia have a limited capacity to process multiple pieces of information at once. When there are five sticky notes in a given area, that may simply be too much information for the person to efficiently process, which would lead them to ignore the notes entirely.

Remembering to take appropriate doses of medication is one of the most important functional skills to preserve in your loved one. If they forget whether they took a medication, they might take another dose, which could result in overdose. On the flip side, if they were to continuously forget to take a medication, they could suffer withdrawal effects or not get the benefit that the medication was supposed to provide. Here are some tips to help your loved one stay consistent with medication:

- Set the alarm on their cell phone or watch to remind them when they're due for a dose of medication. If your loved one does not have a smart device that could be used in this way, consider purchasing the least expensive "smart speaker" available and setting it for them.

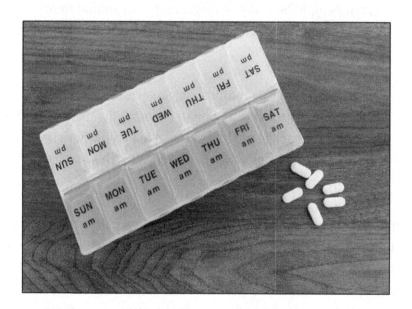

- Buy a weekly pill box that has separate compartments for each day of the week. These are available in most drugstores, and help you track your loved one's pill intake each day. If you notice there are pills in compartments that should have been taken, that could be an indicator that your loved one is forgetting to take their doses. Be sure to monitor this throughout the week, not just at the end of the week. If you are not able to get to your loved one during the day to check, teaching them how to use the video chat function on their phone or computer can be very helpful, as you can ask them to point the camera at the pill box. If possible, have your loved one get used to filling up the pill box on their own. Many families have success with taking a picture of the filled box and keeping it nearby so their loved one can match the pills with the picture. Just be sure to check it regularly for accuracy.

- There are also automated pill boxes that will dispense medication at the correct time and pill boxes that lock, for those individuals who require more help maintaining proper medication management.

- If you are not using a pill box, consider leaving your loved one's medications somewhere easily visible to you as a reminder. Some people find it helpful to turn the pill bottle over when they take their medication so they know they've taken that pill for the day. Again, monitor this to make sure the routine is consistent.

For somewhat complicated tasks, consider writing up a numbered instruction list that you post right near where the activity normally occurs. For instance, if they use email to correspond with their old friends, you might have a list that details how to click on the web browser icon, what bookmark to select, their username and password, and which button to click in order to compose a message.

Overall, focus on reducing the burden on your loved one's cognitive abilities, since everything takes more effort now. Showing them how to group things into categories and organize tasks into individual steps can help them be more independent. Here are a few other tips to consider:

- Set a specific and consistent time of day for certain tasks, like paying bills.

- Organize their workspace, i.e., a place for the mail and bills, a place for keys, a place for completed paperwork.

- Label drawers, cabinets, etc., with their contents if they tend to be confused or overwhelmed when searching for something.

- Provide a large simple calendar with activities clearly marked.

- Provide a list of tasks to be accomplished and check off each task as it is completed.

- Consider installing a large whiteboard in a prominent location in the home where you can write down 2-3 of the most important pieces of information your loved one needs to know for the day, such as when they are being picked up for their doctor's appointment and your telephone number if they need to get in touch.

> **For more resources and strategies, visit our website at recognizingdementia.com**

Treatment of Mood Issues

Just because a person has dementia doesn't mean they can't also be depressed. Mood difficulties and anxiety can often occur with dementia, especially in the early stages when a person may have some awareness that something is wrong. Depending on what the mood issue is, its severity, and your loved one's capabilities, there are many options for treatment. These can include medication for anxiety or depressive symptoms, and supportive counseling for emotional support.

In the past several decades there has been an explosion in the number of medications available to treat mood difficulties. While many primary care doctors will prescribe these medications when elderly individuals show emotional difficulties, the most important thing to do is monitor whether they seem to be effective and determine if they are causing any adverse side effects. For example, benzodiazepines are medications for anxiety attacks that are quick acting but can also be sedating and cause confusion. Often these adverse effects are more severe in older individuals and so they need to be managed carefully.

In regard to antidepressant medications, these can take a month or so to show effects and it may take longer to find the right dosage or perhaps the right medication. The key here is to be patient and communicate with the doctor about what you are seeing. Unfortunately, we often see people who have been taking antidepressants for years and feel that they are adequately treating their depression, but they still feel miserable and exhibit clear emotional symptoms. Sometimes it turns out they haven't let their doctor know how they are feeling and instead respond "Fine!" when the doctor asks.

Be honest and communicate with your loved one's doctor about their mood and symptoms so they can provide the best treatment. If you feel the primary care doctor is not paying adequate attention to your loved one's psychiatric medications, you may consider having them see a psychiatrist, who is a specialist doctor that focuses on treating emotional issues through the use of medication and other medical interventions.

An often-overlooked treatment for mood issues is counseling or psychotherapy. Many people prefer to take a pill, as it seems like a quick fix in comparison to spending an hour in therapy each week. This is also common in older populations that may harbor a stigma about "seeing a shrink." However, clinical research consistently shows that the combination of medication and therapy provides a greater benefit than medication alone. The decision about which interventions are most appropriate for your loved one with emotional issues is going to depend on a few factors. First, what are they willing to do? Doing something about the situation is always going to be better than doing nothing. If they are willing to take a pill for their depression but would never ever step foot in a therapist's office, start there. The other thing to consider is their level of functioning. In individuals with dementia, counseling can sometimes be less effective because they are unable to process what is being said in sessions or they have significant difficulty remembering what was discussed due to memory deficits. Speak with your loved one and don't be afraid to try out different options to see which is the most appropriate for them as an individual.

Behavioral Support

Some individuals with dementia, especially in the later stages or with certain types like frontotemporal dementia, will develop behavioral problems that can be very trying for loved ones and caregivers. These situations often call for the family or caregivers to become more educated about dementia in general and learn techniques to deal with these challenging behaviors. In some cases, more significant interventions may be necessary, such as respite care (temporary professional care of the person to give relief to the typical caregiver) or the use of medication. Frequently, antipsychotic medications are used to help treat the agitation and psychosis (delusions/hallucinations) that can occur in dementia. While these medications can be vital in some situations, they need to be used and monitored carefully since they can have serious side effects. Consultation with your loved one's doctor is always a good first step to start brainstorming solutions to their behavioral problems. Again, the doctor has probably seen many similar cases in their career and can provide some perspective based on other families that have been through it.

Sometimes the primary issue is that a family member or caregiver has a limited understanding of the particular type of dementia that the person has. This is another reason that a full diagnosis and workup is important. Sometimes the caregiver may have unrealistic expectations of the person with dementia or believe inappropriate stereotypes, which can both cause the caregiver to behave in ways that trigger agitation in the person with dementia. In these cases, it can be effective to educate the caregiver on the condition and the triggers that lead to problematic behaviors. For example, in dementia, fatigue and confusion might lead a person to be irritable and resist their caregiver's attempts to help them. Instead of trying to tackle the problematic behavior head-on, maybe you could address the trigger, such as your loved one being hungry, cold, tired, or overwhelmed.

Tips for Dealing with Agitation:
- Don't take it personally.
- Understand that it may not be possible to reason with your loved one when they are agitated.
- Try to remain calm and listen to their concerns.
- Be sympathetic to their underlying concerns and fears.
- Remain positive and distract or redirect your loved one to a preferred activity.

If a loved one does become agitated, remember you can probably not reason with them. This is often true for any of us when we are angry or agitated, but it is even worse for people with dementia, who have poor insight to begin with. Try to remain positive, listen to them, and redirect them to another issue. The distraction and redirection will often be more effective than trying to reason or bargain with an agitated individual with dementia.

If your loved one has some favorite topics or activities, keep them in your back pocket for situations where you might need distraction or redirection. If you loved one enjoys sports, turning on a game might be a great distraction. For other people, food is a surefire way of getting their attention. When someone is agitated or engaging in delusional thought patterns, there is often some sort of fear underneath. For example, we once treated an individual who had the delusional belief that they were going to have to pay for all 10 of their family members to go on a flight to visit them. This was absolutely not the case, but the individual could not be reasoned with and held firm to the fear. When speaking with this person, it became clear that their fear was not the plane tickets, but rather that they were afraid they didn't have enough money. A family member was able to pull up their online banking account and show them there was nothing to worry about financially. This is a great example of side-stepping the immediate issue and instead reassuring and redirecting the person with dementia.

Rather than arguing with the person or begging them to be reasonable, the best course of action is usually to let them know you hear them and will try to take care of the problem. Then try to address their fear or move them toward a preferred activity. For example, if your loved one is agitated because their doctor recently suspended their driver's license due to their dementia, you could reassure them that you know they are upset about how abrupt the change is and you will see if there is anything that can be done. Perhaps you tell them that you are going to go look for the doctor's card to see about giving them a call later. In the meantime, you can turn on their favorite TV show or encourage them to work in the garden for a bit. Often, once the person is able to redirect to another activity, the agitation fades, and they don't remember to follow up on the original concern, which allows you to move on with the day.

Redirection, distraction, or white lies can sometimes feel disingenuous to family members. Obviously, we would all prefer to address things head-on and avoid any hint of dishonesty. However, remember that your loved one may not have the capacity to understand the situation at hand. It is not anyone's fault, and nobody needs to take it personally. These are the unfortunate circumstances of a brain that is not working as well as it used to. The most important thing is to try to help your loved one have a good quality of life and avoid undue emotional hardship. Sometimes that takes creativity on your part and there is nothing wrong with that.

9

Dementia Prevention

There is currently no cure for most forms of dementia. Even though there is a great deal of money and effort being poured into researching possible treatments, unfortunately we may still be years from an answer. Therefore, the best way to intervene is before a dementia condition ever develops. If you'd like to dive deep into a wealth of information about the current suggested strategies for dementia prevention based on available scientific research, we recommend reading Dr. Richard Isaacson's book *Alzheimer's Treatment Alzheimer's Prevention: A Patient and Family Guide*. In the meantime, here are a few important considerations.

We have touched on the fact that the body is one unit and that the health issues that affect you are also affecting your brain. Therefore, one of the most important factors in preventing dementia conditions such as Alzheimer's disease is to manage overall health risk factors such as weight, diet, smoking, cholesterol, blood pressure, and sleep. As with the dementia conditions themselves, there are many chronic health conditions such as cardiovascular disease that lurk under the surface for years before symptoms really start to show. Just because it isn't a crisis yet does not mean it's not important to manage. There is a great deal of personal variation in health, so your default should always be to speak with a doctor before making any changes.

As for exercise, it's a free activity that benefits both your mental and physical health. The bonus is that it can also help prevent dementia. Studies have also shown that exercise helps decrease the amount of amyloid plaque in the brains of rats, which indicates there may be a similar waste-clearing effect in humans. In addition, cardiovascular exercise stimulates the growth of new capillaries in the brain and strengthens the vascular system, helping to keep the brain strong. The research suggests 45–60 minutes of strenuous exercise 3–4 times per week is most effective. However, if you or your loved one is starting from a sedentary baseline or there are physical limitations to consider, don't start off with this recommendation. Instead, gradually work up to it, and avoid all-or-nothing thinking. Any exercise counts, even if it falls short of a particular goal or plan. Here are a few types of exercise to consider:

Exercises for Older Adults:
- Walking or jogging hills in the neighborhood.
- Taking a dance or group fitness class.
- Aquatic aerobics for low-impact cardio.
- Going for a hike.
- Weight training at home with dumbbells or kettlebells.
- Personal training at a local gym.

Diet is also an important component for overall health and the prevention of dementia. The first step should be talking to a doctor about overall health and chronic medical conditions. Going to routine physicals should help them identify any nutritional deficiencies or risk factors that need to be addressed. As with exercise, even subtle dietary changes can make a difference. For instance, if you decide to follow a specific diet, it will still be beneficial to follow that diet four days out of the week, even if you have the goal of following it every day. A 2011 study suggests that eating food high in saturated fat and simple carbohydrates contributes to problematic brain changes that increase risk of Alzheimer's disease. This means that the first things that should be limited or eliminated from someone's diet when trying to prevent dementia are simple sugars such as cane sugar and high fructose corn syrup. Starchy foods such as pasta and rice should also be eaten in moderation, as they quickly break down into sugar as you metabolize them. Rather than simple sugars and starchy foods, try to eat complex carbohydrates including vegetables, whole fruits, brown rice, quinoa, wheat, and legumes. One of the specific diet styles helpful to the brain is the Mediterranean Diet, which follows these guidelines. In the United States, these dietary changes can be difficult to make. The standard American diet tends to be high in saturated fat and simple carbohydrates. We suggest small changes, such as avoiding food and drinks with added sugar, opting for whole grains when possible, and trying to incorporate 1–2 low-carbohydrate meals per day. There are also low-risk supplements that have been associated with decreased risk of developing dementia. As we are not medical doctors, we won't go into detail, but it would be wise to speak with a doctor about supplements such as folic acid, vitamins B12 and D, curcumin, and fish oil with DHA and EPA.

The phrase "stress is the silent killer" was coined to warn people about the effects that chronic stress has on the body. Part of our job as psychologists is to reassure that stress and anxiety can't kill you on a moment-to-moment basis. A panic attack will not actually cause a heart attack or harm you physically. However, over time, the additive effects of stress and anxiety are problematic for your physical health. Stress is designed to help us respond to threats in our environment, but it is not designed to be a long-term state. Studies of mice have shown that stress increases the development of beta-amyloid plaques, which can increase the risk of developing Alzheimer's disease. Anxiety and vulnerability to stress are associated with faster decline in thinking skills and higher likelihood of developing dementia conditions.

All of this is to say that it's important to manage stress if you are hoping to resist Alzheimer's disease and other degenerative brain conditions. Look at your life circumstances and determine whether there are any obvious ongoing stressors that could be dealt with. This is sometimes easier said than done, but making life changes can be more impactful than any particular stress reduction strategy. Consider the scenario of a job where the person is being taken advantage of and has to walk on eggshells to avoid drawing their employer's attention. That is a toxic environment that will cause the person to be under stress near-constantly. This person can learn how to relax their body and think positively, but that does not change the reality of the situation. If they were simply in a different job, they would not be working as much of an uphill battle and could reduce their overall stress levels with techniques and strategies. For additional advice in reducing stress through professional help or self-help strategies, see chapter 13.

Sleep is also tied in numerous ways to dementia conditions. Adequate sleep is an important part of overall health, which means that it is vital for brain health. There are also some interesting things that happen in the brain during the deeper stages of sleep. During deep sleep, your hippocampus (one of the structures affected in Alzheimer's disease) essentially consolidates and transfers your memory into storage. Your dreams may be one aspect of this process. When we see people in our practice who have severely disrupted sleep due to sleep apnea or other sleep conditions, they can show significant difficulties with their memory functioning due to their brains not having the opportunity to effectively store new memories.

Also, during deep sleep, your brain goes through a process called glymphatic clearance. Certain structural cells in the brain shrink back, which creates a pathway for the brain to flush out buildups of abnormal protein. Without good sleep, your brain is not as able to clear these proteins, increasing the risk of developing a degenerative brain condition. The best way to address poor sleep is to practice good sleep hygiene, which is the term we use to refer to behaviors associated with good sleep. If there appears to be a health concern or sleep disorder that is causing lack of sleep, discuss this with a doctor.

Basic Sleep Hygiene Tips:

- Keep a consistent sleep and wake time.
- Have a consistent and predictable pre-sleep routine that focuses on relaxing and unwinding.
- Avoid electronic devices, the internet, and news for about an hour prior to bed.
- Avoid non-sleep activities in bed.
- Avoid daytime napping if it is difficult to fall asleep at night.
- If sleep does not happen after 30–40 minutes of trying, leave bed, engage in a relaxing, unplugged activity, then return to bed and try again.
- Avoid caffeine and other stimulants in the afternoon/evening.

Have you ever heard the saying "use it or lose it"? This is a great mantra to adopt when it comes the brain. If you want to keep a healthy brain over time, keep it stimulated and challenged. Just like you wouldn't expect a muscle to function well by staying completely sedentary, the brain is more likely to develop dysfunction when it is not being stimulated. When people think of stimulating their brain, typically things like crosswords and sudoku come to mind. While these activities are fine and are definitely better than remaining stagnant, they aren't the most effective at increasing your brain's efficiency and staving off degeneration. One of the most effective ways of keeping the brain active is through social activity. It is common for elderly people to become less social and keep to themselves more. This combined with a more sedentary lifestyle does not set the brain up for success. For both young and aging brains, social activity is extremely beneficial. Not everyone is a social butterfly, but things like volunteer activities, regularly scheduled family dinners, social clubs, or a weekly cards group can be perfect ways to continue having regular interactions with other people and getting out of the house each week.

When it comes to mental exercises and brain games, research suggests that they help someone get better at the particular task that they are practicing, but don't do much for overall brain health. Given this, one of the most effective ways to promote a healthy and efficient brain is to instead continue learning new skills. By skills we mean learning how to accomplish a task and building proficiency over time. When you learn a new skill, your brain makes new interconnections, which appears to have a positive impact on thinking skills. There is also a concept called "cognitive reserve," which is basically the brain's resilience to damage. People who accumulate a greater amount of knowledge and skills seem able to hold off brain disease and cognitive decline longer. Learning skills and accumulating more information is a great way to increase cognitive reserve, which can have a protective effect when it comes to the development of dementia conditions. The key point is to find something challenging and enjoyable to do. There are probably millions of activities that involve developing skills, so we can't cover them all. However, here are a few suggestions:

Brain Stimulating Activities:
- Practice another language.
- Learn how to play an instrument.
- Take a dance class.
- Take a computer class.
- Learn knitting, crocheting, or cross-stitch.
- Try out model making.
- Practice photography.
- Take an art appreciation course.
- Learn a new board game or video game.

As of now, these are the most accessible and impactful strategies for preventing cognitive decline and dementia. It's unfortunate that we don't have better solutions for when a dementia condition takes hold, but at least some degree of this is under our control. The important part is being proactive about your brain health *before* it becomes an issue

10

Prognosis: What to Expect

With a positive diagnosis of dementia comes concerns about what to expect. We don't want to sugar coat it. Many forms of dementia are progressive with no identified treatment and will therefore eventually end in the person's death. The expected survival time for individuals with dementia varies depending on the type of dementia and lifestyle factors. Level of care, general health, nutrition, and lifestyle are all major contributors. Despite this variability, it can be worthwhile to learn about the various models that separate dementia into different progressive stages. Even if the stages are broad, most people with dementia follow a common pattern of change. Understanding these stages can be helpful in determining what level of care your loved one might need and in planning for the future.

Stages of Dementia

There are various classification systems used to describe where a person is in the dementia process. The Global Deterioration Scale is a commonly used model that consists of seven stages (Reisberg, Ferris, de Leon & Crook, 1982). The first three stages represent the first signs of cognitive decline and are not yet considered representative of dementia. Someone in Stage 3 of the Global Deterioration Scale would likely be considered to have Mild Cognitive Impairment (as discussed in chapter 2).

Global Deterioration Scale

Stage 1: No Impairment
Functional for age. Normal age-related changes to cognitive abilities. No major impact on life.

Stage 2: Very Mild Decline
Mild complaints about memory, word finding, or other thinking skills with no major functional difficulties in day-to-day life.

Stage 3: Mild Decline (MCI)
Clear deficit in thinking abilities on testing but still able to function normally without major functional decline.

Stage 4: Moderate Decline (Early Dementia)
Progressing cognitive difficulties that are now clear to non-family members. They may live independently but likely have some trouble with complex tasks.

Stage 5: Moderately Severe Decline (Moderate Dementia)
Some assistance is now required. May be able to manage basic daily living activities but should not be fully independent.

Stage 6: Severe Decline (Moderately Severe Dementia)
Assistance likely needed for even basic activities of daily living. Pronounced cognitive issues and behavioral problems are common at this stage.

Stage 7: Very Severe Decline (Late-Stage Dementia)
Requires 24-hour care and assistance with basic needs. Care facilities should be strongly considered at this stage. Ability to walk and verbal abilities may be lost at this stage.

There are numerous other stage models of dementia out there. Rather than going through all of them here, it is most useful to recognize that the development of dementia tends to follow a typical pattern. Below, we will more broadly discuss the general stages of dementia and their characteristics.

How Long Does Each Stage Last? What Are They Like?

The duration of each stage varies depending upon individual characteristics of each person and the type of dementia. That said, some rules of thumb apply. The period of mild dementia (equivalent to Stage 4 on the chart above) often lasts 2–4 years. Most people function fairly independently during this period and may remain in their homes, but lapses in memory are evident and can affect daily life. For example, a person may forget to pay a bill and receive a late charge. In this period your loved one may benefit from you checking in with them and strategizing on how to make sure tasks are carried out. Providing help in setting up a pillbox or a monthly to-do list can be useful.

The middle or moderate stages of dementia (equivalent to Stages 5 and 6 on the chart above) can last anywhere from 2 to 10 years. Cognitive lapses are much more significant in this stage, such as not recalling important information like a home address. Thoughts will become more confused and aphasia may also make it more difficult to communicate. Related to this impairment, behavioral problems and mood issues may become prominent. As this stage progresses, individuals will start to need help with activities of daily life, like bathing and getting dressed. The help required can range from simple prompting and reminders to fully completing the task for them. Independent living will likely not be possible without significant, and possibly full-time, caregiving support. Placing your loved one in a living facility specifically designed for those with cognitive impairment is also sometimes appropriate at this stage.

Some Thoughts on Placing a Loved One:
Placing a loved one in a care facility is a trying experience for everyone. Here are a couple of tips to help with the decision process.

- Remember, there is no one right time to help a loved one transition to a facility, but it is possible to wait too long, resulting in problems and stress for all involved.

- Consider your loved one's mobility issues, wandering and fall risk, their ability to manage medication, healthcare, and home affairs, and an often overlooked, but extremely important issue: caregiver stress.

- When you and your family decide that placement is necessary, a good resource to contact if you are in the United States is your local Long-Term Care Ombudsman's office. This national program provides some oversight of care facilities, placement counseling, and lists of licensed care homes in your area. Just try an internet search for the local office.

- Be aware that the transition process will be challenging and will take time. Don't have unrealistic expectations. Making regular visits to the facility with your loved one before they move in can help ease the process. It can also be helpful to manage and plan the move for them as memory and reasoning difficulties can make it unreasonable for them.

The final stage of dementia (equivalent to Stage 7 on the chart above), in which the dementia has become so advanced that the individual is likely no longer able to communicate with others or participate in their own care, can be quite variable, but often lasts 1–3 years. Individuals at this stage require 24-hour care and may be best helped in a skilled nursing facility due to difficulty moving, feeding, and cleaning them. When a family member or spouse insists that their loved one will never receive care from a stranger, we usually pull them aside and talk about this stage of their progression. Reminding them to take their pills or bathe is one thing. Helping them move, eat, toilet, and perform even the most basic tasks is something else entirely. Not a pretty picture, but this is the reality of the final stages of many progressive dementia conditions.

11

Coping with the Diagnosis

This is an obvious statement to make, but a diagnosis of dementia can be overwhelming for patients and their families. Reactions do differ depending on the individual. Some people take the diagnosis in stride and start immediately planning for action. Others feel numb, confused, disoriented, scared, or even suicidal. Any emotions that come from a diagnosis are normal and many of the scarier reactions are often fleeting immediate responses that quickly dissipate. This is the case for both the individual as well as their family and loved ones. Many people go through this process every day and there are some commonalities in what they experience, which can help in guiding someone through coping with a diagnosis.

Common Experiences

Over the last decade in our clinical practice we have seen a variety of responses to a diagnosis of dementia. Often the responses closely match the stages of grief and loss that are seen with the loss of a loved one. Even though the person who has been diagnosed is likely not going to die soon, the disease may kill them eventually. That's a lot to sit with. Grief can happen when the future that you expected has died. There may be opportunities to have an amazing future full of love and happiness, but the vision of this future without dementia has to go. The person with dementia may also suffer a loss of their sense of self. Being diagnosed with dementia can change one's identity. Some people initially react negatively with denial or anger at what they perceive is an accusation that they are incompetent. This can occur even if the rationale behind the diagnosis is clear and well-documented. This is a little different from someone who may be in the later stages of dementia and have no insight into their condition. Individuals in denial refuse to believe the facts of the diagnosis and may try to "prove" that they are not impaired by refusing help from others. In situations like this, being understanding, patient, and providing gentle education at a pace that the person can tolerate is typically the best course.

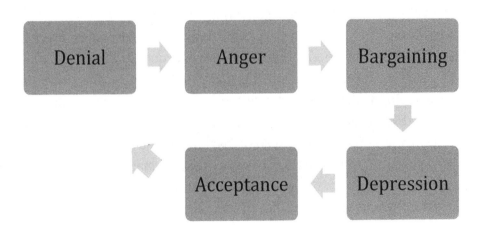

Kübler-Ross Model of Grief

Hopelessness is also a common reaction to a dementia diagnosis. While this is a reasonable response, it tends to result in apathy and an unwillingness to plan or act. It's normal for people to engage in catastrophizing, which is the psychological term for when someone takes a piece of bad news or information and escalates it into a full-blown crisis in their minds. Of course, a person with progressive dementia will eventually become quite impaired, and that's definitely not happy news.

But the truth is that they don't instantly become severely impaired and unable to live a happy life. There may still be a great deal that they can experience, accomplish, and enjoy. Just like the response to full denial, the most appropriate action from the family is to provide loving support, gentle education, and appropriate challenging of those irrational beliefs that might be causing the person to throw in the towel prematurely.

Although we have just described two problematic response styles, in our practice we have found that many people have a more calm and reasonable response that can lead to action. As we mentioned, grief is a normal aspect of being diagnosed with dementia. Although it may seem odd, grief can help us move on. Allowing yourself to experience the stages of grief can allow you to make peace with the changes and move forward in a positive way. It is important to respect each person's individual expression of grief. When possible, provide emotional support and quality time with your loved one. If they seem to be funneling their emotions about the diagnosis into developing an action plan and doing everything they can to make sure they have researched every aspect of their disease, just know that it may be a positive way of coping instead of dwelling on the saddest aspects of their diagnosis. At the same time, be aware that the stages of grief are not always predictable, and someone might suddenly change from motivation to despair. If you find that your loved one seems to be stuck in a difficult grief reaction, professional support can be beneficial.

Frustration is also a common reaction. This can be positive or negative depending on the situation. Sometimes people will become frustrated at a specific issue, such as the fact that more cannot be done by doctors, or a specific deficit, like their word-finding difficulty. Occasional frustration can be healthy when it encourages someone to act on their situation. If your loved one seems to dwell and become consumed by their frustrations, there may be cause for concern. Some individuals become so angry that they refuse treatments, become belligerent with their doctors, or project their anger and frustration onto their loved ones. When this type of frustration and anger occurs, it is often better to avoid reasoning with the person and instead simply listen and be supportive. They may just need to vent and be heard before they are able to engage the more reasonable part of their mind.

The last response to a dementia diagnosis that we want to mention may be surprising. After we have a feedback session with someone and explain their testing results that reveal a dementia condition, they often thank us and express relief. Why relief? Well, the person feels that they are finally heard. It can be reassuring to know there actually is something going on and you're not just imaging the difficulties that bug you on a daily basis. Sometimes people express concern that others in their life have downplayed their deficits or have been afraid to talk with them about the changes they have seen. For these individuals, receiving the diagnosis is a validation of their experience and it helps them understand that it is not their fault.

A person can experience any of these responses or all of them at various points following a diagnosis of dementia. It will likely be an emotional and apprehensive time. Also, please remember that these responses can be experienced by both the individual with dementia and/or by their family and loved ones. Try to be understanding and supportive to everyone involved. For more information and caregiving tips, check out the Alzheimer's Association's guide at https://www.alz.org/help-support/caregiving.

Coping Strategies

Everyone copes in a different way and will likely move through at least some of the stages of grief in the wake of a dementia diagnosis. However, there are some strategies that can help you move forward in a more productive fashion. One is to channel any frustration, fear, or anger into useful action or at least planning your response. Make an effort to avoid sitting and ruminating on worries. Throwing yourself into dealing with dementia can be a protective factor itself. The three strategies we suggest to individuals with dementia and their families are to focus on seeking support, educating themselves, and planning for the future.

1. Seek Support

When it comes to supporting a loved one with dementia, many people feel that their love and care will be enough to help them. Unfortunately, we are only human, and despite our best intentions, going it alone is often not successful in the long run. A better approach is to be aware that at some point, you may need help in caring for your loved one, and it is better to identify the sources of such help now, rather than when you are totally overwhelmed.

The internet makes it very easy to find local support services and even see how they are rated. One good first stop is the website for the Alzheimer's Association (www.alz.org). Most areas of the United States have a local Alzheimer's Association chapter and offer support groups, information on new research and clinical trials, and case managers who can help you find whatever support you're looking for. Don't be fooled by the name: they help with all sorts of dementia, not just Alzheimer's. Many other types of dementia also have organizations you can look to for support. In addition, a lot of communities have local caregiver support groups or comprehensive caregiver wellness centers. In our area, we are lucky enough to have a great caregiver wellness center, which we refer most of our patients to because they have support groups, caregiving classes, and a resource library. While not every region is going to have extensive caregiving resources, do your due diligence and identify the resources that are at your disposal. Caregiver support groups are an amazing, and often under-utilized, resource. They offer a great way to connect with others who are going through similar situations, which helps you to realize that you are not alone. There are certain things that you are inevitably not going to want to talk about in front of your loved one, or there might be concerns you don't want to burden your family with. Having a group of people who are also going through provides an environment to express those concerns without guilt. Support groups also allow you to get advice about how to deal with certain behaviors from your loved one. For instance, if your loved one is at the point where they should no longer be driving, but you are scared of taking their car away, you might be able to get some strategies that worked out for other families.

Another important tool to be aware of is respite care. As a caregiver, it is easy to become exhausted and experience "caregiver burnout." It's such a common problem that we devoted chapter 13 of this book to the topic. Respite care is basically when you temporarily hand off the caregiving duties for your loved one to a professional. This can take the form of in-home help or checking your loved one into a facility for a few days. It can give both of you a much-needed break, which helps to support the health of the caregiver and to improve the relationship between you and your loved one with dementia. In a similar vein, many communities have what are called adult day care or adult day health programs. These are usually half-day activity programs for people with dementia. Many programs will even pick your loved one up from their home before taking them to their facility or on an outing with their peers. Meals or snacks are typically included in day programs as well. This can help you, as a caregiver or family member, maintain your sense of self and avoid falling into the common trap of devoting 100 percent of your time and energy to caregiving while ignoring your personal needs. It may seem counterintuitive to some, but getting some distance from your loved one can actually make you a better caregiver.

2. Learn

When we give trainings about dementia, one of the first things we do is ask people to give their definitions of dementia. It turns out dementia is one of those things everyone has heard of and believes they understand. However, when you look at the definitions people give, there are some widely varying ideas. Educating yourself about dementia in general and the specific type of dementia your loved one has can help you comprehend what is happening and be more understanding. The good news is you have already taken the first step in this process by reading this book!

Learn about the particular type of dementia your loved one has, its common issues, and the treatments for it. While the internet is an amazing resource, it can also be misleading, especially in regard to treatments for dementia. Progressive dementia conditions are terrifying, and we all want to do whatever we can to avoid our loved ones declining and losing their abilities. Unfortunately, there are many unscrupulous people who are willing to take advantage of that fear. If you read about a treatment that sounds too good to be true, chances are it is. Do extensive research with reputable sources, and consult your loved one's doctor, before engaging with any sort of treatment. There are also amazing online communities such as Alzheimer's Universe (alzu.org), which provide discussion boards and resources to help guide decision making.

3. Plan for the Future

This strategy may seem obvious, but it is often overlooked. When someone receives a diagnosis of dementia, it is time to start considering long-term goals and desires. This means considering some potentially uncomfortable decisions about care and other issues that many of us would like to put off until we must face them. However, remember that every person wants to retain their dignity and independence as long as possible. By planning for the future early on and throughout the progression of their dementia, you may be able to help them remain independent longer.

We suggest having open and honest conversations with your loved one soon after the diagnosis. This doesn't need to happen on the way home from the doctor's appointment, but it's best to not procrastinate on these talks. Remember that there will not necessarily be one big talk where the entire rest of your loved one's life will be determined. It will be a series of big and small, casual and serious talks that occur over the following years. During your early conversations, the goal should be to consider your loved one's wishes and preferences. Perhaps there are certain experiences or "bucket list" items that they would like to take part in while they still can. Start gauging your loved one's feelings about where they see themselves living, and don't make assumptions. We have encountered families that assume their loved one with dementia wants to fight tooth and nail to stay in their home while their disease progresses, only to find out that the person is actually relieved to downsize and have some things taken care of by the staff of a living facility. In these talks, you may want to develop a rough outline in your head and some specific criteria that would indicate when a change in care or living situation is called for. This isn't a binding contract, but a means to ease into these difficult topics early on so nobody is surprised down the line. Whenever possible, involve your loved one with dementia in these decisions and get their input. This will help prevent them feeling as though their rights and choices are being stripped away from them.

When planning for the future, consider consulting with an attorney who focuses on elder issues. They can assist with creating a will, managing your loved one's estate, establishing end-of-life plans, appointing power of attorney, or beginning the conservatorship process if necessary. These issues can be quite complex, so we suggest you leave it to the professionals.

Planning for the future is particularly helpful to the caregiver for several reasons. It allows you to feel more prepared and less overwhelmed when your loved one eventually needs a higher level of care. It also allows you to make financial arrangements and be certain that additional assistance is going to be available. Most importantly though, planning for the future will help the caregiver maintain their identity in the relationship with their loved one. Have you ever met someone caring for a spouse who now seems more like a nurse than a husband or wife? It is easy to get sucked into the caregiver role to the loss of your other roles, like child or spouse. By planning for the future, including arranging for additional caregivers when needed and planning activities for yourself with your loved one outside of the care needs, you are more likely to retain the roles you want to maintain.

12

Living with Someone
Who Has Dementia

In the previous chapter we focused on how to cope with a dementia diagnosis. Now we look at how to maintain a pleasant relationship with a loved one who has dementia. So, let's explore some of the most effective ways to interact with your loved one as their symptoms become more prominent. We will discuss ways in which you can modify or improve the home environment to help the individual with dementia and what we can do to improve their capacity to be successful. Finally, we will focus on the most important thing to remember throughout this journey: Despite whatever limitations or symptoms a person may present, they are still the person you love, and you can figure out what they need. Behavior is a form of communication, the trick is just in interpreting that behavior and what your loved one is trying to indicate to you through their actions.

Environmental Issues

Some of the easiest ways to help people with dementia don't involve their cognitive abilities. As we age many of us start to experience a loss of sensory abilities, such as hearing and vision. Hearing loss in particular can be a major contributor to apparent memory loss. Even if your loved one doesn't struggle with hearing, there are changes you can make to their living environment that may make things easier for you both. And a little patience will go a long way in making your time together more enjoyable.

Unfortunately, we all probably have older relatives who don't like to wear their hearing aids or forget to put them in. This can be worse with dementia. Individuals with dementia may struggle to identify vision or hearing loss as an issue, so they will not speak up about problems or may see no need to use hearing or visual aids. Instead, these individuals may isolate themselves or become more passive in conversations. To start with, get their senses professionally checked out. Even stubborn older adults sometimes respond to a person in authority, such as their physician, telling them they need to use those hearing aids.

Besides encouraging your loved one to use compensation devices like hearing aids and reading glasses or magnifiers, there are other simple changes you can try to help them absorb information more effectively. Have you ever tried to have a conversation with someone while they are focused on something else? Like an important project or an engaging television show? I (Dr. Lande) have seen this in myself when I'm driving. It seems that invariably when I am in heavy traffic and focused on figuring out where I am going, one of my children brings up something important they want me to do, like sign a paper for school or help them find a missing toy. And half the time at least I forget it by the time I get home. My children don't though, and instead they blame me for having a bad memory given that I didn't remember something they consider so important. Obviously, when they wait to discuss important things with me when I am not focused on something else, I do better.

None of us are as good at dividing our attention as we would like to think, and this is even more apparent in individuals with dementia. Remember that people with dementia often have difficulty understanding what is said to them and comprehending language in the way they used to. This is part of that symptom called aphasia. This means that getting your point across to them may be somewhat of an uphill battle. Add in trying to talk to them in a noisy environment with many distractions, or when the television is on and they are trying to eat breakfast, and you can almost guarantee the person is not going to fully process what you are trying to tell them. To get the most out of communication with your loved one, try to speak with them when there are few distractions. If there is something important to discuss, consider moving to another location, turning off the television, or making sure they aren't in the middle of some other activity. Once you have a more conducive environment for communication, make eye contact with your loved one and try to use short, simple phrases to get your point across.

Our world has become extremely fast paced and always connected. It is just about inevitable that any household will have numerous gadgets and electronics to facilitate getting things done quickly and moving on to the next task. This does not bode well for success in working with someone who has dementia. This is where patience comes in. In fact, patience underlies many of the strategies we are discussing here. Taking your time and allowing for trial and error will nearly always be better than rushing through tasks and getting frustrated when the pieces don't fall into place the way you expected. With this in mind, let's discuss some other ways you can work with your loved one to improve their day-to-day functioning.

Basic Capacity

When spending time with your loved one, especially when trying to discuss something important, remain aware of their interest and mood. It is hard for any of us to reason effectively if we are upset. In individuals with dementia, their overall communication skills may already be reduced, which makes this effect even more prominent. It's not unusual for someone with dementia to become prone to "shutting down" and ceasing communication altogether.

It's common for individuals with dementia to become overwhelmed and agitated more quickly and easily than normally functioning people. This

157

can look like the person becoming flustered, red in the face, or even adopting aggressive body posture like an animal backed into a corner.

If this happens, the last thing you should do is try to convince them they are wrong or overreacting. It probably wouldn't work on you in such a situation and it definitely won't work on your loved one with dementia. Instead, your first duty is to help them calm down. You can try some simple clarification, but if that's not working, move on and plan to return to the issue later when they are in a better position to talk. Once they are in a calmer location, the goal should be redirection. Let them know that you hear them, and you understand their frustration, but try to help move them toward focusing on something else. Sometimes a simple distraction, like suggesting a snack or asking them to wait a few minutes while you go use the restroom, is all it takes to get their focus off what is distressing them. Other times, their agitation may be so high that you need to reiterate that you care about what they feel, and you hear what they are saying, while you wait for the intense emotions to subside.

Tips for Communicating with People Who Have Dementia
- Speak slowly and simply.
- Limit the length of meetings (15–20 minutes is better than an hour).
- Ask one question at a time.
- Give plenty of time for a response.
- If he/she does not understand, think of another way to word things.
- Use frequent repetition and question your loved one to make sure they understand.
- In simple terms, explain what you want to accomplish.
- Discuss ideas in terms of their goals rather than yours.
- Do not argue or try to excessively reason with your loved one.
- Do not take cruel words or inappropriate actions personally.

So now that you have your loved one in a good emotional state and you've addressed any environmental problems, like a noisy room, let's discuss some basic strategies for improving your loves ones' capacity to be successful.

On the next page is a list of straightforward ideas. The key point is to simplify information, confirm it is being taken in, and to try different ideas if your strategy is not working. You can also help them maintain focus by providing important information in verbal and written format, or by prompting with non-verbal gestures when you are speaking.

Reasoning with and Understanding Dementia

Spending time with a loved one who has dementia can sometimes be a very frustrating or upsetting experience. Witnessing someone decline in their thinking abilities and overall functioning is no fun, but their changes in behavior and difficulty communicating can make the experience even harder.

A key point that we would like you to remember is that all behavior, no matter how bizarre, is a form of communication. In people in the more advanced stages of dementia, communication can be significantly impacted, and their behavior becomes one of the most important clues to understanding their needs and fears. Your job as a loved one is to remember this, and to remember that their behavior is appropriate to their level of brain health and functioning, even if it doesn't fit within society or your family's standards. Try to not take their actions personally. Instead, ask yourself what underlying concern the behavior is trying to communicate.

If you've ever raised children, you've already engaged this skill. When an infant is hungry or needs a diaper change, they don't calmly request, "Excuse me. Would you please change my diaper?" They cry. Sometimes they scream bloody murder. That behavior is their form of communication.

159

As you continue trying to interpret the child's behavior, you start to become more tuned in to their behavioral language. You might learn the difference between a hungry cry, an ouchie cry, and a middle-of-the-night cry while the kid is fully asleep. The point here is not to suggest that adults with dementia are like children, but it does provide a nice basis for comparison. The goal is to understand what is triggering the behavior and what the behavior might be communicating, and determine what can be done to help your loved one with the situation.

Another point to remember is that when our loved ones have trouble communicating with words due to dementia, they are just as likely to have trouble comprehending what we are saying. Negative behaviors sometimes result from the individual with dementia misunderstanding the situation. This is where those hints in the Communicating with Dementia chart become really important. Also be aware of what your behavior is communicating to them. If you become angry or aggressive, they may respond similarly or withdraw and become frightened of you. Don't take their behavior personally. It is the dementia acting through them.

> "To understand is to forgive"
>
> - Blaise Pascal

Remember that most negative behaviors are reactive. The individual with dementia, who may have trouble with reasoning or communicating, is likely reacting to either a situational or internal stressor. For example, we are often asked to consult at skilled nursing facilities about patients with moderate or worse dementia who won't stop yelling and groaning. They appear fearful, confused, or perhaps in some discomfort. We have found that in some cases a review of the medical chart indicates this is an individual who has had many years of chronic pain. Now, they are no longer able to ask for pain medications, or perhaps even realize why they are upset, so they call out. In these cases, switching to regularly scheduled pain medications instead of relying on the person to ask for them can be helpful.

Learning your loved one's behaviors and reactions to daily situations can be like learning a new language. For this reason, you might want to take notes or even keep a specific notebook that focuses on their behavior and communication abilities. When an incident occurs, write what happened just prior, what your loved one's reaction was, how you played into the situation, what was happening in the environment, and what your guesses are as to what the behavior *meant*. This is a great way to track tendencies over time, and to figure out what sort of actions are most helpful in helping them cope with similar situations.

Particular issues to consider when behavioral problems arise include physical discomfort, such as pain, hunger, or being cold, as well as general fatigue. It can be easy to forget that when someone's brain is not functioning properly, they will get tired and overwhelmed more easily. They may not be able to handle the day-long party when all of the relatives come for Thanksgiving. That does not mean your loved one can't participate at all. But be aware of their possible limitations, and try to take breaks and intervene before they become overwhelmed. With individuals who have more advanced stages of dementia, it can be better for them to be at the family get-together but have a room to the side for them to relax in a calmer setting. They can retreat there alone if they need to, or sit there and spend time more quietly with just one or two family members at a time. If you get frustrated by your loved one's behavior, try to remember that their actions represent their current level of brain function. We don't expect young children to handle themselves quietly and with dignity when there are 20 people coming to their home for a holiday party. Instead, we monitor them and support them. We give them breaks when needed. We treat our loved ones with dementia in a similar way.

13

Taking Care of Yourself
as a Caregiver

This chapter is dedicated to you. As someone who is likely a family member, friend or caregiver of someone with dementia, it is massively important that you don't forget about yourself and your own needs. The Family Caregiver Alliance estimates that family members provide 80 percent of elderly care. A 2015 report by AARP estimates that caregivers spend an average of 24 hours per week providing care. People who live with the affected individual spend an average of 41 hours per week providing care. The problem is that caring for someone we love with dementia can be a full-time job, and you may already have a regular full-time job or children to care for. When our loved ones develop a condition like dementia, it is easy to become so involved in their care and managing the day-to-day issues that occur that we lose sight of our original relationship with the person. Suddenly the person feels more like a patient than a loved one. Further, you can start to lose your relationship with yourself and lose sight of who you are beyond a caregiver. This role confusion can be damaging to your relationship with the person you are caring for and it is easy to become burned out by all the work and roles you are trying to fill. Burnout means that you become frustrated, tired, and irritable. It also probably means that you are starting to be a less effective caregiver. The good news is that there are strategies that you can use to prevent caregiver burnout and to address it once it has started to take root.

Be Proactive

Let's be more specific about what burnout exactly means. In this context, we're focusing on caregiver burnout, but you can burn out in a variety of other contexts such as with work or school. Typically, burnout feels like you want to throw up your hands in surrender and just be left alone. It can be difficult to concentrate and keep working on tasks. The dictionary definition of burnout is a "physical or mental collapse caused by overwork or stress." Being a caregiver for anyone, let alone someone with dementia, can result in stress and being overworked, but the term "collapse" is what really matters here. It's a type of physical and/or mental exhaustion where you will start to stumble in your duties, make errors, lose track of your identity and needs, and even start to resent or be angry toward your loved one, as they might seem like the source of all the hardship you are experiencing.

Burnout Warning Signs
- Exhaustion or lack of energy.
- Irritability and/or sadness for no obvious cause.
- Withdrawal from others.
- Getting sick more easily.
- Changes in appetite and sleep.
- Drinking more.
- Difficulty concentrating.
- A short fuse or mood swings.
- Avoiding your loved one.
- Feelings of resentment toward your loved one.

Burnout is something that we are all at risk of. It is not a matter of not being dedicated or loving enough. This is so important to remember. It is not due to a lack of care on your part. Instead, it is caused by factors that are often outside of your control. As a caregiver for someone with dementia you can try to be prepared and try to have a schedule, but sometimes things will just fall apart in ways you couldn't have predicted. This is because you are dealing with a living, complex person, made somewhat more complex and unpredictable by their dementia. Other issues, such as lack of support from others, and work/regular life imbalance also contribute to burnout. Here is a chart of warning symptoms so you can catch it in yourself before you become burnt out.

Be Compassionate... Toward Yourself

Now that you recognize the symptoms and causes of caregiver burnout, let's discuss how to prevent it and deal with it when it occurs. One area caregivers struggle with is setting realistic goals and knowing their own limits. Even superheroes have their limits. You don't need to do everything. Taking on the burden of caregiving might mean changing some other things in your life or saying no to responsibilities that you previously managed. Maybe this is the year you finally let someone else host the big family holiday party. Even if your sister is going to do a subpar job that does not begin to compare to your shindig-throwing skill, it might be more important to focus on making sure that your mother is adequately cared for during the party so that everyone can have peace of mind.

Part of knowing your limits may include making some changes in activities that you and your loved one enjoy doing. A new factor to consider when making plans is the fatigue level of both your loved one and yourself. Predicting fatigue in your aging loved one may be a no-brainer, but you might be surprised at how much caring for someone with dementia can take out of you. Don't try to pull through an activity or task just because you think you should be able to. Take breaks as needed and don't be afraid to cancel or postpone an activity if it's not feasible. The goal is to avoid becoming unduly overwhelmed. Often coming back to the activity later when you are refreshed can make things more enjoyable and more efficient for everyone.

It is also essential to get some alone time. Yes, you are caring for a loved one with significant needs, but you are a person, too. In addition to making time for your normal chores and life activities that are unrelated to caregiving, take leisure time for yourself. It's okay to go sit outside and enjoy the sun, spend time with your friends, go see a movie, or take a small vacation. Taking time for yourself is caring for yourself, which can help you give better care to your loved one. If you have other family who can assist with the caregiving or take over your normal duties from time to time, it can help in multiple ways. For one, it can help the other people in your life have a more realistic appreciation for what you do every day. Caregiving is not an easy job! It may also be nice for your loved one to have a little variety and spend some time with other people. It's normal for both you and your loved one to get a little sick of each other from time to time. If you don't have family or friends who can help out, remember that respite care is another option. There are likely facilities or organizations in your area that would be able to take over caregiving for the weekend while you go clear your head (and maybe have a glass of wine).

Besides taking time away from caregiving, engaging in frequent self-care activities is another effective means for staving off caregiver burnout. Self-care is a broad term that refers to activities that are physically or mentally healthy, and that can help give you some buffer to better withstand stress and emotional hardship. This can mean everything from keeping up with your doctor's appointments to making sure you get adequate nutrition, exercise, and engage in activities that you find fun and relaxing. Try not to get hung up on engaging in the "perfect" self-care activities. Take exercise for instance. Research suggests that 45 minutes of strenuous cardiovascular exercise multiple times per week has significant mental health benefits. That might be unrealistic given your lifestyle and all your other responsibilities. That's okay. Any exercise is better than no exercise.

165

Maybe you could make a point to take a long walk three times per week or do some heavy work in the garden while your loved one naps.

Relaxation is another important self-care activity to consider. Although it sounds simple, relaxation might be more essential than you realize. When you get stressed by something unexpected or dangerous, your body goes into a stress response. Perhaps you've heard of the "fight or flight response"? It's the body's natural reaction to threats. Your body prepares for immediate action by speeding up your heart and breathing rate, creating tension in your muscles, and slowing down the less important functions having to do with repair and recuperation. This response is great for jumping out of the way when a car is about to run you over or for protecting yourself from a home invader. But it's not meant for long-term responding. The fight or flight response wears your body out. When the stressor doesn't go away, you might find yourself running ragged as your body tries to keep up its defenses. Luckily, as humans we also have a built-in mechanism for resting and recovering—you just need to learn how to tell your body to switch modes.

Since the fight or flight response is not sustainable forever, our bodies also have a counterpart called the relaxation response. This basically does the opposite of the fight or flight response. It slows down your bodily functions, creates a sense of calm, and helps your body recover. The trick to kicking off this relaxation response is breathing. Obviously, we all know how to breathe, but have you ever noticed that you can tell when someone is sleeping by the way that they breathe? When you are asleep, you tend to take slow belly breaths, engaging your diaphragm. This is the kind of breathing that promotes that restorative relaxation we are looking for. During the day, especially when under stress, we tend to only use the upper portion of our lungs. You can observe this by breathing normally while holding a hand on your chest and a hand on your stomach. Now try to imagine breathing into your lower abdomen and stomach area. As you breathe in, let your stomach expand and then continue filling air into your

166

chest and upper lungs. This is diaphragmatic breathing. It's also used by singers when they are trying to get enough air to adequately supply the notes they are making.

Taking a few deep diaphragmatic breaths may feel good and can help to ease some tension, but to effectively use breathing as a tool to engage that relaxation response and get the deep repair your body needs, it takes practice. There are many different types of breathing exercises that you can do to help you take these deep breaths in a systematic way. Our favorite is an extremely simple exercise called 4-7-8 breathing. All you do is breathe in fully, filling your lungs for 4 seconds, hold that breath for 7 seconds, and then exhale completely for 8 seconds. Repeat this process until you feel the deep relaxation start to take root in your body. Depending on your comfort level, you can count faster or slower. This exercise should not be straining for you, so adapt it to be comfortable for your body if necessary. Find a relaxing space, sit or lie comfortably, and spend 2–5 minutes engaging in breathing exercise to feel the full benefits. If you want to get the most bang for your buck, you may want to practice your breathing exercises during times when you aren't already stressed or anxious. This is just like practicing any other physical skill such as throwing a football or doing a back handspring. You are going to want to practice and train the skill on your own so you can count on it when you're under pressure. If you never practice your breathing exercises and teach your body what it feels like to engage that relaxation response, you may not be able to rely on the skill when you are in a stressful situation.

Humans are social animals and truly caring for yourself is not just about independent self-care activities. You need support from others, too. Even if you tend to be more introverted and isolated, being with others allows us to get out of our own heads and absorb ideas from other people. When you spend so much time managing your own responsibilities and also needs and wants of your loved one, it is easy to become isolated and let social connections slip away. Make sure you are not going through this alone. Reach out to your family, friends, other caregivers, or even look toward professional help.

Even if you don't have time for a phone call or text, many of us can eventually get around to answering an email or social media post. Besides this direct communication, the internet also lets us search for others who are going through what we are experiencing. It lets us share a common experience. We have already mentioned in-person support groups that are available for caregivers. In addition, there are many online communities and groups on social media that serve a similar purpose. Even if you aren't able to be in the physical presence of others, perhaps due to a lack of resources in your area, online resources help you understand that you are not alone in the struggles that come along with caring for someone with dementia.

Helpful online support groups:
- Alzconnected.org has online forums for both caregivers and for people that have Alzheimer's disease.
- Dementia Care Central has a great list of online support groups at https://www.dementiacarecentral.com/caregiverinfo/careforcare givers/support/
- You can also search "dementia" in the search bar of Facebook, then click on Groups to find lots of helpful groups focused on dementia support.

To finish up this section, let's return to our overall topic of remembering to be compassionate not just to those we are caring for, but to ourselves. Caregivers are often warm and compassionate people who are understanding of others when they fail or make mistakes. That grace doesn't always extend to the caregiver themselves. In Western culture, we have a strong focus on success, perfection, and self-esteem. We don't like to admit that we have weaknesses or occasionally fall short of our goals. If you are going to make it through the process of being a caregiver for someone with dementia, you must develop some self-compassion. Give yourself the same grace you would give someone else in your position. When you fail or run into roadblocks, instead of getting angry, dwelling on self-criticism, or ignoring the issue, work toward acceptance. You are human and none of us are perfect. You will lose your temper at some point. You will say something you regret. You will question whether you are good enough to care for your loved one. Maintaining self-compassion means that we try to acknowledge these truths and be kind to ourselves in the moment. It's not about avoiding responsibility; it's about doing what needs to be done to keep yourself afloat and continue moving forward. Good self-compassion can be difficult to achieve, but research has shown that it reduces stress and has many of the same mental health benefits as the good self-esteem we have all focused on for so long. If this concept has grabbed your attention and you, we would like to learn more about it, we recommend the book *Self-Compassion* by Kristin Neff, Ph.D.

The last topic we'd like to discuss related to taking good care of yourself is therapy. Even though we have made a lot of progress in the discussion of mental health over the past few years, when people hear therapy, they still often have a negative association. They might think of lying on the couch talking about their mother while an old white guy with a beard nods and asks, "How does that make you feel?" While that experience is still available, therapy these days often looks much different. Most modern mental health providers (therapists or psychologists) do therapy that is much more active. It will look a lot more like collaborative problem solving. The therapist will listen to your concerns, ask clarifying questions, and help you to think of solutions or different ways of looking at your situation. If you are interested in pursuing therapy for yourself, you do not need to have a diagnosed mental disorder. Simply go to psychologytoday.com or look up your local "psychological association" and use their search tools. This service is often covered under your insurance, so you may have access to free or reduced cost support.

If you'd like more detailed tips on finding a mental health provider in your area, Dr. Duff has a tutorial at duffthepsych.com/findatherapist. For free bonus videos, including tips for caregiving over the holidays and avoiding scams that target the elderly, visit recognizingdementia.com/bonus.

14

Conclusion

Congratulations! We're proud of you for making it through this book and confronting some possibly difficult truths. The process of learning about dementia, considering where your loved one stands, and taking steps to address issues is NOT easy. We hope this book gave you the information you needed at this leg in your journey. Putting in this effort will serve you and your loved one well.

We did our best to be accurate and helpful, but it's important to remember that the information presented within this book is a starting point. If there is any topic we presented that is particularly interesting to you, we encourage you to dive deeper. There are numerous books, in-person and online classes, local resources, videos, blogs, and more that can help you expand your knowledge about these subjects. Dementia is a complicated and ever-evolving topic, but now you have a strong framework to build upon.

Don't be a superhero and don't try to be your loved one's doctor. If you find that the information we presented about symptoms, diagnoses, or issues surrounding dementia conditions ring true, take the information and collaborate with your loved one's medical team. If they don't have a medical team, establish one. Leave the clinical work to the professionals.

Focus on being well-informed and taking great care of yourself and your loved one. If you have questions or doubts about the way your loved one is being cared for, voice them. If you suspect your loved one may be suffering from one of those pesky conditions that can masquerade as dementia (like chronic urinary tract infections), let them know. You are now in a much better position to collaborate with the doctors and be an active part of your loved one's care network.

If you enjoyed this book, please consider leaving an honest review on Amazon or on whatever platform you purchased the book from. Reviews not only help the book succeed, but people look to reviews to understand what the book is about and whether it could be beneficial for their situation. It's important to us that this information reaches the people who need it. In addition to writing your honest review, if there is someone you think would benefit from this book, please consider sharing a relevant chapter or quote from it so they can decide if it would be worth their time.

Thank you again for taking the time to read this book. We wish you the absolute best on your journey.

Glossary

Acetylcholine: A neurotransmitter (chemical signal used by neurons to communicate with other neurons) often involved in memory and movement.

Alzheimer's disease: A type of cortical dementia marked by disorientation, memory loss, and language difficulties. The most common form of dementia.

Amyloid plaque: The buildup of clumps of Beta-amyloid that is damaging to neurons.

Aphasia: A general medical term meaning impaired language skills. It can indicate problems with receptive language, expressive language, or both.

Apraxia: A motor problem in which a person can not perform certain acts even though they know how to do so.

Aricept: A medication used to treat dementia. It works by maintaining the amount of acetylcholine (a neurotransmitter involved in memory) in the synapse between neurons.

Basal ganglia: Structures deep within the brain involved in movement, emotion, and cognition.

Beta-amyloid: A protein fragment that builds up in the brain in individuals with Alzheimer's disease and is damaging to neurons.

Cerebrovascular accident (CVA): Also known as a stroke. Death of an area of the brain following impaired blood flow. Can be caused by blockages or rupture of a blood vessel.

Cerebrovascular disease: Various conditions that limit blood circulation in the brain, causing damage to brain tissue.

Chorea: An involuntary condition in which a person suffers from uncontrollable jerky movements that can appear almost dance-like.

Chronic traumatic encephalopathy: A degenerative brain disease caused by a history of repetitive head trauma. It has been associated with some sports, such as football. It is rare and causes impaired thinking and impulsive actions.

Cortex: The outer layer of the brain. The bark or gray matter. It is involved in awareness and many thinking skills.

Cortical dementia: Dementias associated with degeneration in the cerebral cortex. Alzheimer's disease is an example.

Corticobasal degeneration: A form of subcortical dementia, involving damage to basal ganglia and marked by movement difficulties and impaired thinking abilities.

Creutzfeldt-Jakob disease: A rapidly progressive and fatal cortical dementia. It is marked by impaired memory, behavioral changes, and vision and coordination difficulties.

Crystallized intelligence: Well-learned knowledge and skills, such as vocabulary.

Delusions: Beliefs that are not in touch with reality and are often held despite evidence contradicting them.

Dementia: A clinical syndrome. It describes a person's level of functioning and indicates that a person has serious impairment in thinking skills and a decline in functional skills (daily activities) or independence. Typically used to describe degenerative conditions in older people. It is acquired and represents a decline in functioning.

Denial: Declaring something to be untrue. To be unwilling to accept. Sometimes confused with loss of insight in individuals with dementia conditions.

Dopamine: A neurotransmitter involved in movement and fine motor control. Loss of dopamine producing neurons is implicated in Parkinson's disease and Lewy body disease.

DSM: The diagnostic and statistical manual of the American Psychiatric Association. It provides diagnosis guidelines for dementia and other psychiatric conditions.

Executive functions: A term used to describe a class of thinking skills that relate to goal directed behaviors. It includes skills involved in determining a goal, making a plan to accomplish the goal, initiating action, ignoring distractions, multi-tasking, and reasoning.

Fluid intelligence: The ability to reason and solve new problems without needing previously learned knowledge. Deductive reasoning would be an example of this.

Frontal lobe: A section of the brain, in the front specifically, responsible for movement and deciding to move, which includes reasoning and decision-making. It controls our behavior and is involved in emotion, personality, reasoning, concentration, and memory.

Frontotemporal degeneration: A type of cortical dementia in which brain deterioration starts in the frontal and/or temporal lobe. Depending upon the area in which it starts, the first areas of impairment generally involve behavioral changes or language problems.

Hallucinations: A form of loss of touch with reality in which a person experiences sensory experiences that are not real. Such as hearing voices or seeing something that is not really there. It differs from a delusion in that it is not just a belief, the person has the experience of witnessing the false voice or image. Can also be smells or tactile sensations.

Hippocampus: A structure in the brain, deep in the temporal lobes, that is responsible for memory formation. It acts as an index. Without it, people do not form new long-term memories. It is damaged in conditions such as Alzheimer's disease.

Huntington's disease: A subcortical form of dementia marked by mood changes, cognitive impairment, and motor dysfunction that includes jerky movement called chorea.

Insight: Awareness. Understanding the true nature of one's condition.

Intelligence: The ability to build knowledge and skills and then to apply and use them.

Lacunar infarct/stroke: An ischemic stroke caused when a small artery that penetrates deep into the brain is blocked. It causes a small cavity of dead space and can result in some movement or sensory difficulties at times.

Levodopa: A precursor chemical the body can change into dopamine. It is used as a primary treatment for conditions such as Parkinson's disease.

Lewy body disease: A form of dementia marked by fluctuations in cognitive difficulties, mild movement difficulties, and visual hallucinations. It is related to dopamine loss and buildup of Lewy bodies in the brain.

Major neurocognitive disorder: Created to replace the term dementia. Significant cognitive impairment that interferes with functional skills and independence. It is acquired, represents a decline from previous functioning, and this term was meant to be more inclusive, including younger adults as well as older.

Mild cognitive impairment (MCI): A description of functioning meant to characterize people showing serious cognitive impairment, but no significant functional difficulties or loss of independence. It is a risk sign for possible later worsening to dementia.

Mild neurocognitive disorder: Created to replace the term "mild cognitive impairment." It describes significant cognitive decline that does not severely affect functional abilities or independence, though some compensation strategies may be needed. It is acquired and represents a decline in functioning.

Mixed dementia: A combination of several types of dementia, often resulting in a faster progression of deficits. A common combination is Alzheimer's disease with vascular dementia.

Multiple system atrophy: A subcortical dementia marked by loss of mobility and movement, as well as problems with autonomic systems such as blood pressure.

Myelin sheath: Fatty tissue that surrounds and protects the axons of neurons, also improving transmission of nerve impulses. It can be disrupted by conditions such as multiple sclerosis.

Neurodegenerative: Something that causes or is related to loss and degeneration of neurons.

Neurofibrillary tangle: Clumps of tau protein and portions of neurons seen in Alzheimer's disease and some other diseases. They interfere with neuronal functioning.

Neurologist: A physician who studies the brain and nervous system and who often is the primary treater of dementia conditions. Although like psychiatrists they are working with the mind, they focus on the physical side.

Neuron: A brain cell that brings in sensory information or sends out motor information. It is the basic component of the nervous system and brain.

Neuropsychologist: A type of psychologist who specializes in understanding and treating disorders that relate to how the brain and behavior interact.

Occipital lobe: A section of the brain, at the back, responsible for processing visual information.

Parietal lobe: A section of the brain, toward the middle and top, responsible for tactile and sensory information, as well as mapping the space around you.

Parkinson's disease: A degenerative condition related to the loss of neurons that produce dopamine. As a result, motor control becomes weakened and difficulties such as tremor, rigidity, and difficulty walking may develop. Some individuals with Parkinson's will show cognitive impairment marked by slowed processing and difficulty with complex information.

Parkinson's plus condition: A group of degenerative conditions that include Parkinson's as part of each condition, but also additional forms of impairment. For example, Lewy body disease, multiple system atrophy, and progressive supranuclear palsy.

Parkinsonism: A clinical syndrome marked by tremor, postural problems, rigidity, and slow movement. It is the manifestation of Parkinson's disease.

PET scan: A type of functional brain imaging scan. It uses tracers to evaluate how the brain is functioning. For example, it can be used to evaluate metabolism or observe the accumulation of amyloid plaque.

Processing speed: Speed of information processing in the brain. It means how quickly the brain can take in and work with information.

Progressive supranuclear palsy: A degenerative subcortical condition that affects walking, balance, and the ability to move one's eyes. It is a Parkinson's Plus condition.

Psychiatrist: A type of physician who specializes in mental health. Although like neurologists they are working with the mind, they focus on the emotional side.

Psychosis: Loss of contact with reality, can be marked by significant confusion, agitation, delusions, and/or hallucinations.

Senile: Means something caused by advanced age. In the past "senile dementia" was used to describe cognitive impairment that was thought to be part of the aging process. With advances in medicine it is now understood that this was not normal aging, but instead reflected degenerative diseases.

Small vessel ischemic disease: A group of conditions also known as white matter disease, including microbleeds in the brain, lesions in the white matter, and lacunar infarcts (small empty spots caused by a small artery bleed), that reflect damage to the cerebrovascular system and so contribute to cognitive decline.

Stroke: Also known as a cerebrovascular accident. Death of an area of the brain following impaired blood flow. Can be caused by blockages or a rupture of a blood vessel.

Subcortical dementia: Dementias associated with degeneration of the subcortical regions of the brain. Parkinson's dementia is an example.

Synapse: The space between two neurons though which they pass chemical messages.

Tau: Proteins that give structure to neurons. In Alzheimer's disease they become defective.

Temporal lobe: An area of the brain, on each side, responsible for auditory processing. The hippocampus, responsible for memory formation, is located deep within it.

Traumatic brain injury: An injury to the brain caused by some sort of bump or jolt. The skull may or may not be damaged. The injury results in an alteration in consciousness of varying length depending upon the severity of the injury.

Vascular dementia: A form of dementia caused by stroke or excessive cerebrovascular disease. Deficits from it depend upon the area damaged.

Visuospatial skills: The ability to accurately perceive and understand visual objects and spatial relationships, such as how to draw or build something.

White matter disease: A group of conditions also known as small vessel ischemic disease, including microbleeds in the brain, lesions in the white matter, and lacunar infarcts (small empty spots caused by a small artery bleed), that reflect damage to the cerebrovascular system and so contribute to cognitive decline.

About the Authors

Erik Lande, Ph.D.
Jargon, rushed appointments, and just general lack of communication with doctors frustrates us all when we are concerned about our health, or that of our loved ones. One of the most important goals I have as a neuropsychologist is to listen, understand my patient's concerns, and provide realistic recommendations to help them. I think it is important to put things in terms that we can all understand. I try to keep this in mind with all of my work, both clinical work and teaching.

Currently, I work as a neuropsychologist at Insight Neuropsychology in Camarillo, California. I also lecture in the Counseling, Clinical, and School Psychology graduate program at University of California, Santa Barbara and provide consultation and training to local groups, including Adult Protective Services, Crisis Intervention Training for law enforcement, and the Ombudsman's program. Besides my clinical work, I am kept busy running to karate and swim lessons for my three boys. I reside with my wonderful wife and my boys in Ventura County, California.

Robert Duff, Ph.D.
This book represents my attempt to bridge the gap between my work as a neuropsychologist at Insight Neuropsychology and my passion for making mental health content "for real people." Unexplained jargon and inaccessible resources nearly led to tragedy in my own life, which caused me to begin a personal crusade to make content that speaks to you like a real person. In addition to my clinical work, I am the author of the best-selling *Hardcore Self Help* book series and the host of a podcast by the same name. I live in Ventura County, California with my wife, dogs, and two crazy boys. Outside of work, I love playing video games, watching superhero movies with the family, and having long conversations about life over a few glasses of red wine.

Acknowledgments

We have to start by thanking our wonderful wives and families. We really couldn't have finished this project without their support. Joelle Duff assisted particularly with graphic design and getting our website up and going. Kate Lande was also there with a ready ear to bounce ideas off. Both of them got to read drafts ad nauseum. To our children, thanks for putting up with all the times we said to let us finish one more page before we leave for the park, or karate, or school...

We would also like to thank Ella Morton, who really helped us out and kept us on track with suggestions and editing services. To our Beta readers, like Rick Wanlass, Marcy Snider, Lynn Jones, Sarah Belgard, Victor Espinosa, Cary Hardy, Jim Moens, and Daniel Bradley, thank you for your honest feedback and helpful comments.

We would also like to thank all the professionals that we have collaborated with over the years. Thank you for your efforts and the expertise that you have so generously shared with us. Finally, thank you to the patients that we have worked with over the years. You have been our greatest teachers, and this project would not have been possible without you.

References

2. What is Dementia?

...one out of every three seniors will have some form of dementia at the time of their death; more than five million Americans currently have Alzheimer's disease.
Alzheimer's Association. 2018 Alzheimer's Disease Facts and Figures. Alzheimer's Dementia 2018; 14(3):367-429

A 2013 study conducted at the Rush Institute for Healthy Aging in Chicago estimated that the number of people with Alzheimer's disease will climb to over 13 million by 2050
Hebert, L. E., Weuve, J., Scherr, P. A., & Evans, D. A. (2013). Alzheimer disease in the United States (2010-2050) estimated using the 2010 census. Neurology, 80(19), 1778–1783.

It is currently estimated that about 5–25 percent of older adults have MCI and the incidence increases as they age
Petersen, R. C., Lopez, O., Armstrong, M. J., Getchius, T., Ganguli, M., Gloss, D., ... Rae-Grant, A. (2018). Practice guideline update summary: Mild cognitive impairment: Report of the Guideline Development, Dissemination, and Implementation Subcommittee of the American Academy of Neurology. *Neurology, 90*(3), 126–135.

The Alzheimer's Association estimates that medical care for individuals with dementia costs over $287,000 on average during the last five years of their life. Beyond that, families end up spending a great deal of their time caring for the individual with dementia. In fact, caregivers in the United States provide approximately 18 billion years of unpaid care each year.
Alzheimer's Association. 2019 Alzheimer's Disease Facts and Figures. Alzheimers Dement 2019;15(3):321-87.

3. Normal Aging

There is a hypothesis put forth by people like Robert L. West (1996) that explains why this decrease in fluid intelligence happens in older adults while their crystallized intelligence remains mostly intact. It's called the Frontal Lobe Hypothesis and it essentially claims that the frontal area of the brain tends to age more quickly than the other parts of the brain.
West, R. L. (1996). An application of prefrontal cortex function theory to cognitive aging. *Psychological Bulletin, 120*(2), 272-292.

5. Types of Dementia

Dementia caused by frontotemporal degeneration is less common than that caused by Alzheimer's disease, accounting for somewhere between 5 and 10 percent of dementia cases

Alzheimer's Research UK, https://www.alzheimersresearchuk.org/about-dementia/types-of-dementia/frontotemporal-dementia/ftdabout/

...between 60 and 80 percent of all dementia cases are attributed to the effects of Alzheimer's disease.
Alzheimer's Association. 2019 Alzheimer's Disease Facts and Figures. Alzheimers Dement 2019;15(3):321-87.

9. Dementia Prevention
A 2011 study suggests that eating food high in saturated fat and simple carbohydrates contributes to problematic brain changes that increase risk of Alzheimer's disease.
Schiöth, H. B., Craft, S., Brooks, S. J., Frey, W. H., 2nd, & Benedict, C. (2012). Brain insulin signaling and Alzheimer's disease: current evidence and future directions. *Molecular neurobiology, 46*(1), 4–10.

Studies of mice have shown that stress increases the development of beta-amyloid plaques, which can increase the risk of developing Alzheimer's disease.
Justice, N. J. et al. (2015). Posttraumatic Stress Disorder-Like Induction Elevates β-Amyloid Levels, Which Directly Activates Corticotropin-Releasing Factor Neurons to Exacerbate Stress Responses. *Journal of Neuroscience,*35(6), 2612-2623

10. Prognosis: What to Expect
The Global Deterioration Scale is a commonly used model that consists of seven stages
Reisberg, B., Ferris, S. H., de Leon, M. J., & Crook, T. (1982). The Global Deterioration Scale for assessment of primary degenerative dementia. *The American Journal of Psychiatry, 139*(9), 1136-1139.

13. Taking Care of Yourself as a Caregiver
A 2015 report by AARP estimates that caregivers spend an average of 24 hours per week providing care. People who live with the affected individual spend an average of 41 hours per week providing care.
National Alliance for Caregiving and AARP Public Policy Institute. (2015). Caregiving in the U.S. 2015.
https://www.caregiving.org/wp-content/uploads/2015/05/2015_CaregivingintheUS_Executive-Summary-June-4_WEB.pdf

Image Credits

3. Normal Aging
Inzitari, D., Pracucci, G., Poggesi, A., Carlucci, G., Barkhof, F., Chabriat, H., ... LADIS Study Group (2009). Changes in white matter as determinant of global functional decline in older independent outpatients: three year follow-up of LADIS (leukoaraiosis and disability) study cohort. *BMJ* (Clinical research ed.), 339, b2477.

5. Types of Dementia
Klunkwe, CC BY-SA 3.0, https://commons.wikimedia.org/w/index.php?curid=5470244

6. Conditions That Can Look Like Dementia
Blausen.com staff (2014). "Medical gallery of Blausen Medical 2014." *WikiJournal of Medicine* 1 (2). CC BY 3.0,
https://commons.wikimedia.org/w/index.php?curid=31118595

Anderson, M.M. (1986). Normal pressure hydrocephalus. *British medical journal, 293 6551*, 837-8 .

7. Working with Doctors for a Diagnosis
CT: Case courtesy of Dr. Andrew Dixon, Radiopaedia.org,
https://radiopaedia.org/cases/elderly-ct-brain

MRI: Novaksean, CC BY-SA 4.0,
https://commons.wikimedia.org/w/index.php?curid=44348140

EEG: Der Lange, CC-BY-SA-2.0,
https://commons.wikimedia.org/w/index.php?curid=845554

PET Scan: Jens Maus (http://jens-maus.de/), Public Domain,
https://commons.wikimedia.org/w/index.php?curid=404690

Made in the USA
Las Vegas, NV
07 May 2022

48571655R00105